EUROPEAN

NAVAL

AND

MARITIME

HISTORY,

300–1500

EUROPEAN

NAVAL

AND

MARITIME

HISTORY,

300–1500

Archibald R. Lewis
and
Timothy J. Runyan

INDIANA UNIVERSITY PRESS
BLOOMINGTON

Manufactured in the United States of America

Lewis, Archibald Ross, 1914—
  European naval and maritime history, 300–1500.

  Bibliography: p.
  Includes index.
  1. Navigation—Europe—History. 2. Europe—History, Naval.
  I. Runyan, Timothy J. II. Title.
VK55.L48 1985   387.5'094   84–48485
ISBN 0–253–32082–8

SE

For Betty and Laurie

CONTENTS

Illustrations

Maps

Preface

THIS VOLUME OCCUPIES a special place in maritime history since it represents a first attempt on a popular level to present an overall survey of the rich, diverse, and exciting development of European naval and maritime power during the Middle Ages. Though a number of general surveys exist which deal with the navies and shipping of antiquity, except for the excellent though highly technical recent book by Richard Unger, *The Ship in the Medieval Economy* 600–1600, such surveys are lacking for the thousand years which represent medieval times.

Interestingly enough, we are best served for the early Middle Ages, where a number of volumes, mainly written in English and dealing with the Mediterranean and the northern seas of Europe, carry the story down to 1100. From the time of the Crusades, however, we find ourselves in serious difficulties. True, we have several excellent histories of Venice. We have the scattered books and articles that give us some picture of Genoese sea power, especially in the last years of the medieval period. We possess a few articles concerning Amalfi. But until we reach the end of the period we have to rely almost entirely upon an older and inadequate picture of Italian sea power written in Italian or upon the recent volume by Hocquet, which is in French.

Similarly, except for a handful of books on the Catalans after 1200, we can find little to help us in assessing the role of the important sea power of Catalonia and of the Aragonese Empire in general. We are equally without a guide when we try to discover the nature of the navies of the Kingdom of Two Sicilies. Further, no specialized studies exist at all concerning the navies of the Muslim dynasties, or those of southern France in the western Mediterranean, or of the Ayyubid or Mamluk flotillas in the eastern Middle Sea. So we have found ourselves cast adrift in these southern waters without a scholarly pilot to guide us.

In the northern seas of Europe, there exist similar gaps in scholarship. The only study in English of Hanseatic sea power is the translation of Dollinger's work. And English medieval navies and shipping have been examined only in a few scattered articles or in out-of-date surveys by Nicolas and Brooks except for the later Middle Ages. As for French navies, we must still mainly rely on a disappointing older survey, while there are no studies in English of the seapower of post-Viking Scandinavian monarchies at all. Indeed, only Portuguese naval developments have been adequately studied, and they suffer from the fact that few comparisons, except in embryo form, can be made with the sea power of nearby Castile. In writing this book, then, its authors have frequently had to make bricks without straw in the hope that what they have to say will be approximately correct and will stimulate further research. They must beg the reader's indulgence for the obvious *lacunae* in their narrative.

Secondly, the authors hope that the reader will understand that they are construing naval history as including maritime and commercial relationships as well, rather than as a simple listing of naval actions on the sea. There are certain reasons why they have done so. First, during these centuries no clear distinction existed between naval forces and merchant shipping. Trading ships were pressed into naval service by every kind of sea power examined in these pages—sometimes on a *regular* basis in the cases of Scandinavia, England, Byzantium, or Venice and Genoa. And second, warships were often used to carry commercial cargoes in time of peace or, in the case of Mediterranean galleys, even in time of war. A distinction between merchant ships and naval vessels, then, though it did exist at times, seems to be an essentially modern distinction inappropriate to the medieval period, when most ships were both, often at the same time. In mingling the naval with the maritime commercial elements, the authors are not unaware of how incongruous these two elements may seem to some of their readers, but insist that this mingling represents a reality that it would be wise for them to accept.

Finally, a word about the ship types which are described in these pages. Though many previous authors, especially prior to Unger, have presented an apparently clear picture of various types of ships in use during these centuries, the authors are less sure about such classifications than some of their predecessors were. Recent research and, especially, evidence from naval archeology have emphasized that it is impossible to describe ship types with any real precision. There never was anything like a "typical" *navis*, or long ship or galley, or *cog* or *carrack*. Instead, ship types were not only constantly modified in myriad ways through the passage of time, but tended to blend into one another during the same period as well. The same ship might even be called by quite different names, depending upon who is referring to it. To describe ship types is a convenient oversimplification of reality, useful only as long as it is clear that it represents only an approximation of this reality and little more.

In writing this volume, the authors hope that both the scholarly and non-scholarly reader will appreciate that they have frequently sailed into dangerous waters, where the shoals of their ignorance are a constant threat and where their scholarly navigational instruments are very much hit-or-miss. It is their hope that the reader will grasp why they have insisted on lumping together naval and commercial merchant shipping activities. And they trust that most of their readers will understand that the types of vessels they describe are not as distinctive or as different from one another as one would conclude from reading earlier volumes on the subject or even their own prose. And may all that they say about this subject be regarded as provisional and subject to revision when the next few underwater wrecks are carefully examined by experts.

BOOKS ARE NOT WRITTEN on topics so far-reaching as this one without incurring debts. The authors would like to recognize the assistance of Professors John

Dotson (Southern Illinois University), Michael Altschul (Case Western Reserve University), and James Gillespie (Cleveland, Ohio) for their suggestions on the improvement of the text in its various stages of preparation. For their suggestions on a number of points and advice on illustrative material we are grateful to Lionel Casson (New York), Ole Crumlin-Pedersen (Roskilde), Ian Friel (Geenwich), Richard Steffy (Texas A + M), Barbara Kreutz (Bryn Mawr), Richard Unger (Vancouver) and Chjristiane Villian-Gandossi (Paris). Bernard Bachrach (University of Minnesota) encouraged us in the project from its inception. We have availed ourselves of the opportunities at two major gatherings of scholars of maritime studies to present our interpretations as well as engage in exchanges with others. The Naval History Symposium, held at Annapolis at the U.S. Naval Academy in alternate years, is a stimulating conference that attracts students of ships and the seas from around the world. The North American Society for Oceanic History, which convenes at important maritime centers annually, brings together knowledgeable and stimulating participants whose interests readily encompass our enthusiasm for early maritime history.

EUROPEAN

NAVAL

AND

MARITIME

HISTORY,

300–1500

CHAPTER I

The Late Roman World to A.D. 500

WHEN OCTAVIAN DEFEATED Anthony and Cleopatra at the naval battle of Actium in 31 B.C. and in doing so gained control of the Roman Empire and of the entire Mediterranean Sea, a new era began. This naval action ended more than half a millennium of strife, during which hostile fleets had struggled for mastery of the waters of the Middle Sea. Such fleets—Phoenician, Greek, Carthaginian, Hellenistic, or Roman, or even flotillas of corsairs from Cilicia or other pirate lairs—had periodically disturbed the peace in various areas of the Mediterranean and Black seas. They had helped to decide the destiny of the peoples who lived along these shores and also developed a whole set of specialized warships and naval tactics.

Now, as Octavian became the Emperor Augustus and his victorious squadrons mopped up after victory, and in doing so completed what Pompey's pirate suppression campaign had begun two decades earlier, a single naval power controlled the sea from the Pillars of Hercules to Egypt, Syria, and the Propontis. By this time nothing challenged Rome in Atlantic waters either, for Julius Caesar had ended the sea power of the Venetii of Brittany by conquering Gaul. And though Britain had to wait until the reign of the Emperor

1

Claudius to fall to Rome, neither its inhabitants nor the even more primitive Celts of Ireland or Scotland possessed the ships or the maritime skills capable of threatening Roman-held shores.

Nor did the Teutonic peoples who lived along the coasts of Frisia, northern Germany, or in Scandinavia represent any threat to the Romans in a maritime sense, as archeologists have shown in examining their ships. Their vessels were small, oared craft without sails which could travel only along the coast close to shore or in inland waters like the Baltic, the Kattegat, and the Skaggerack. For instance, when Augustus's general Varro lost his legions to Arminius in the Teutoberg forest of Germany in A.D. 9, there is no evidence that his defeat resulted in a German threat of any consequence on the waters of the North Sea.

Similarly, when Augustus decided to exert his authority over client kingdoms in Thrace and Asia Minor, there is no evidence that he faced any naval opposition in the waters of the Black Sea. Even the Red Sea near Egypt, which he had made his personal domain after Cleopatra's death, seems to have been peaceful. No organized naval opposition to Rome existed in either the Mediterranean, the northern seas of Europe, the Euxine (Black Sea), or the Red Sea. Rome's internal and external maritime traffic could sail everywhere undisturbed.

Thus unchallenged, Augustus proceeded to organize the empire's naval establishment in a way which was to last almost three centuries. The Roman Imperial fleet of oared warships, much reduced in size from what it had been during the civil wars of past decades, was now based in two ports in Italy. One of these was at Misenum near Naples, the other at Ravenna. Its principal duty, beyond the suppression of piracy, seems to have been to see that the great grain fleets, which carried free wheat and olive oil from Egypt and North Africa to feed the swollen populace of Rome, reached their destination at the mouth of the Tiber undisturbed. Probably it is for this reason that the admiral in charge of the imperial fleet made Misenum his headquarters. As for the naval base at Ravenna, it had a long history and continued to be of strategic importance. Its location permitted convenient access to timber and naval stores which were available along nearby shores of the Adriatic.

Were there smaller squadrons of patrol ships located in other parts of the Mediterranean-Black Sea area which were controlled by local Roman governors who ruled imperial or senatorial provinces? It seems probable, though our information concerning such squadrons is scanty indeed, except in the case of Herod's port of Caesarea in Palestine, which is now being carefully examined by Israeli maritime specialists. All we can say with assurance is that in the Middle Sea the *Pax Romana* prevailed down to the last decades of the third century and that our sources mention no naval actions taking place in these waters which disturbed this peace.

In waters beyond the Middle Sea, there is evidence of somewhat more naval activity on an *ad hoc* basis, especially during those years when Britain was conquered and Frisia absorbed by the Julio-Claudians and when Scotland was invaded by the Antonines and by the Severi, who succeeded them as emperors. There is no evidence, however, that this activity resulted in any permanent Roman naval establishment of consequence in Atlantic or northern waters. Instead, it seems clear that commercial shipping pressed into service provided Roman armies with the naval support they occasionally needed in the Irish Sea, the Channel, or the North Sea during these years. Similarly, along the Rhine and the Danube rivers as well as in the Black Sea, during campaigns waged against barbarians in the second and third centuries, the Romans relied upon river fleets pressed into service on a temporary basis for the duration of these campaigns and not on permanent naval forces.

What effect did these informal arrangements have upon naval technology and tactics and upon naval organization in general? Though recent excavations have revealed that the Romans constructed a great artificial harbor near Ostia to handle the large volume of grain shipped to the capital and improved a number of harbors elsewhere in the empire such as at Leptis Magna, as noted earlier, they seem to have neglected other aspects of naval technology during these centuries. Since they needed no large warships to patrol the Middle Sea, they did not build them—even though the fact that they did construct some huge grain ships shows that they possessed the necessary technical skill to do so. Their neglect of naval tactics was due in part to their very success in creating the long peace which prevailed on the sea. It was an all but moribund imperial naval system which survived in the Mediterranean by the third century. The same was true in non-Mediterranean waters during the time when Scandinavia was enjoying its so-called Roman iron age. Nothing more was necessary.

Then came that dreadful third-century crisis, which from the end of the Severi in 235 to the time of Diocletian in 284, saw the empire almost disintegrate. Constant civil strife between regional claimants to the imperial throne destroyed the classical empire of Augustus and Hadrian and ushered in a new state of affairs. How did this upheaval affect the Roman world's maritime and naval situation?

In the first place, we note that these years saw the end of the empire's freedom from outside naval assault. Goths and their allies in the east used the waters of the Black Sea to attack Roman shores and even sailed their ships into the Aegean, though it must be admitted that they were more active in raiding the Balkans and Anatolia by land.

More serious was the maritime situation in the west where, for the first time, Irish and Pictish pirates began to attack the shores of Britain. They were joined by Saxons, who raided in the North Sea and in the Channel. Not only was Frisia abandoned, thus losing the empire the site for a valuable naval base, but for a brief period Carausius, using naval power, was able to maintain himself in Britain as a usurping island emperor. By the time a series of able emperors had managed to restore order late in the century, it was a very different Roman world which faced the future.

What direct naval and maritime changes resulted from all of this turmoil in the Mediterranean-Black Sea world? Very few. There was no return to even the limited naval establishments which the Julio-Claudians, Antonines, and Severi had so long maintained in this part of the world. And since neither Persians nor barbarians had managed to establish themselves permanently along Mediterranean shores, there was no special reason for the imperial government to feel threatened in the Middle Sea from a naval point of view.

On the other hand, there is considerable evidence that important changes began to take place in these waters which were to play a vital indirect role in their long-range future. The first of these was the movement of the empire's capitals during the reigns of Diocletian and Constantine. The city of Rome ceased to be an imperial capital in the west by the early fourth century, to be replaced first by Milan and then by Ravenna as the residence of western Augusti or emperors. At the same time, Trier in the Rhinelands was chosen as a sub-capital, where western Caesars, who were the chief assistants of these emperors, lived.

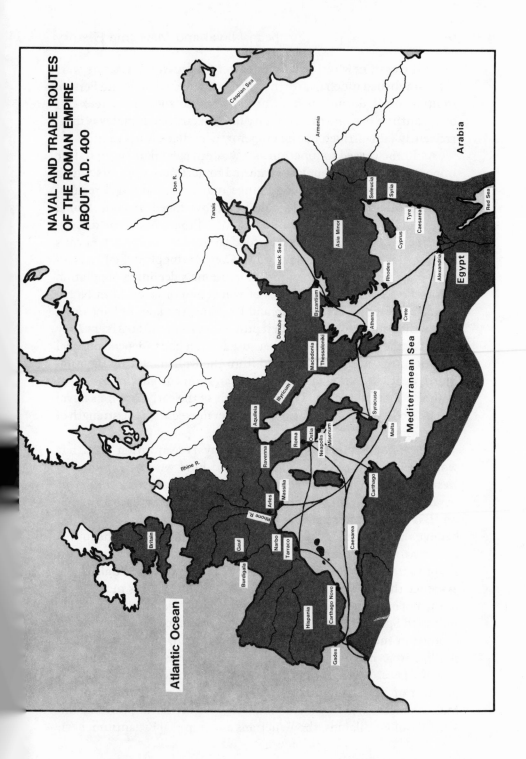

NAVAL AND TRADE ROUTES
OF THE ROMAN EMPIRE
ABOUT A.D. 400

Atlantic Ocean

Mediterranean Sea

Caspian Sea

Arabia

Egypt

Red Sea

Armenia

Syria

Seleucia

Tyre

Caesarea

Cyprus

Rhodes

Asia Minor

Alexandria

Crete

Athens

Byzantium

Thessaloniki

Macedonia

Black Sea

Tanais

Don R.

Danube R.

Illyricum

Aquileia

Ravenna

Rhine R.

Roma

Ostia

Neapolis

Misenum

Syracuse

Malta

Carthago

Caesarea

Arles

Massilia

Rhone R.

Narbo

Tarraco

Gaul

Burdigala

Britain

Hispania

Carthago Novo

Gades

In the east, new residences for eastern Augusti and Caesars were also established much nearer the sensitive lower Danube and Persian frontiers until, during the reign of Constantine, the small Greek city of Byzantium became the great city of Constantinople and was magnificently embellished by the emperor, who made it his capital.

As Rome ceased to function as a western capital, it began to lose importance, and its population started to decline—a process which had both immediate and long-range maritime and naval results. Neither Milan nor Ravenna could be provisioned by grain which reached Ostia and the mouth of the Tiber. Nor could Constantinople's special new need for food be ignored. As a result, Egypt's surplus grain began to be shipped to Constantinople, which was, of course, closer to Egypt than to Rome. Rome's declining population had to be content with supplies of wheat and olive oil from North Africa and Sicily. As for Milan and Ravenna, the laws of Diocletian reveal that they had to draw their provisions from the Po River valley and from the general Adriatic area, just as Trier had to depend on local supplies from northern Gaul and from the Rhinelands. By the mid-fourth century, that great Mediterranean grain current linking Egypt with the Tiber, which had been the basis of the early Empire's naval responsibility and organization, no longer flowed with the strength of earlier times.

We cannot be sure how this affected naval organization, though it would seem that naval flotillas of some kind were maintained in western Mediterranean waters to assure the safety of grain ships sailing from Carthage and other Tunisian ports to Ostia. Probably such flotillas were based in part in North Africa. We also have reason to believe that other new flotillas were built in the course of the fourth century to assure the peaceful provisioning of Constantinople with supplies from Egypt or from the nearby Black Sea areas. We also have evidence that in the fourth century a second flotilla was maintained in the upper Adriatic with Istria as home port to insure communication with Split, where Diocletian had his residence, or with imperial capitals in the Po Valley. And it is interesting to note that all these flotillas were based in areas such as the Adriatic, the Propontis, or North Africa, where timber resources were especially abundant. A pattern of maritime strength was beginning to appear in the Mediterranean, which was to result later in the naval power of the Vandals and Aghlabids, the Venetians and Imperial Byzantium, even though we still have little evidence that true naval power had as yet appeared in any of these locations.

Though few *direct* naval changes had as yet appeared in the Mediterranean-Black Sea area by the mid-fourth century, we do begin to find a new pattern of naval defenses in the more distant Roman provinces facing the Atlantic and the North Sea. These defenses consisted of a number of fortified ports and coastal bases situated along the North Sea and Channel coasts of Britain from the Humber to Portsmouth. According to the early fifth century list of Roman officials, the *Notitia Dignitatum*, these ports and bases were controlled by a military official known as the *Count of the Saxon Shore*. A second set of naval defenses was located along the western coast of Britain on both sides of the Bristol Channel and near Chester just north of Wales. Finally, near Boulogne and along the Channel shores of Gaul as far west as Brittany, a third set of defenses was established which were also controlled by local Roman military commanders.

Were these Roman naval defenses active or passive in nature? In other words, were they coordinated with an active fleet which patrolled these waters? We do know from our sources that Roman officials used what are described as "Pictish" ships to defend these coasts—which has been interpreted to mean that they used vessels which were swift scouting ships, or which were ships painted or camouflaged like those of the Picts, or which were built along lines similar to those used by the Picts when they raided Roman Britain.

On the whole, however, it seems wiser for us to conclude that Rome's naval defenses in this part of the western empire, like her land defenses, were passive rather than active, and that she did not maintain a large fleet able to carry the war at sea to her Irish, Pictish, or Saxon naval opponents. Our reason for saying so lies in the fact that in the fourth century, after northern Britain had been overrun by Picts, who seem to have bypassed the Antonine Wall by sea, a series of new watchtowers was built along the North Sea coast from Newcastle to the Humber. Had the Romans an active fleet and a policy of using that fleet against naval enemies in the north by raiding their shores, such defenses as those built in Yorkshire would have been totally unnecessary. That they *were* built presupposes an imperial naval policy in this part of the world which was essentially passive and similar to that policy which used flotillas along the Rhine and Danube rivers to protect imperial boundaries, but which relied much more on interior

Roman wine boat with six oarsmen (although 22 oars are shown),
master, and helmsman. The third-century sculpture was found at
Neumagen and is now at Trier, where such vessels worked along
the Rhine River. By permission of the Rheinisches Landesmuseum,
Trier, West Germany.

mobile land forces to contain an attack once it had been launched and
had reached deep into Roman territory. Thus, it seems clear that by
the late fourth century, the Roman Empire had failed to develop
sufficient naval forces either in the Mediterranean or along Atlantic
shores to protect itself from real or potential enemies. Instead, it still
relied mostly upon its army, on foot or on horseback, deep in Roman
territory to give it a secure defense.

Then came the disastrous years between 378 and 500, when the
empire in the west collapsed under the attacks of barbarians from the
north and northeast. How did these attacks affect the empire's naval
forces? And did they result in any changes in the use of such forces as
already existed? In short, did the barbarian invasions of the Roman
world result in any significant naval changes in the Roman Empire,
east or west?

On the whole, the answer is again a negative one, an answer which
can best be explained by examining just how these invasions took

place. They began in 378 when the Visigoths, who while fleeing from victorious Huns were allowed to cross the lower Danube in force, defeated the legions of the Emperor Valens at Adrianople. Contained in the Balkans until 395 by the military skill and diplomacy of the Emperor Theodosius, after his death they resumed their raids along the middle Danube until the eastern Emperor Arcadius sent them west to attack his brother, the western Emperor Honorius, in northern Italy.

The Visigothic invasion of Italy led to the sack of the city of Rome in 410 and eventually to Visigothic settlement in southwestern Gaul. It also forced western Roman military authorities to weaken their armed forces in Britain and along the Rhine so that they could defend the Po River valley. As a result, a number of barbarian tribes were able to breach the Rhine defenses of the empire and penetrate deep into Gaul and Spain. By 439 Franks, Burgundians, and Alemanni had taken over parts of Gaul, and Vandals had reached southern Spain, from which they were driven into North Africa by Visigoths, who were invited to do so by local Roman authorities. As a result, the Visigoths became the rulers of most of the Iberian Peninsula while maintaining their rule in southern Gaul.

In summary, by the mid-fifth century, when things were briefly stabilized in the west by the Roman *magister militum*, Aetius—a man who was able to muster a joint Roman-Barbarian army and defeat Attila and his Huns at Chalons—a large part of the western Roman Empire was in barbarian hands: Franks, Alemanni, and Burgundians in Gaul; Visigoths in Spain and southern France; and Vandals in North Africa. Roman elements still ruled Italy, and most of Britain and parts of northern Gaul were still controlled by local Roman leaders independent of Ravenna; but the empire in the west had ceased to be a viable force for the defense of its inhabitants on either land or sea.

When we examine these invasions of the continental domains of the Roman Empire, one point stands out. All the barbarian peoples whom we have mentioned arrived at their final destination by land routes. With the possible exception of the Suevi, who began their migration on the southern shores of the Baltic Sea and who may have reached northwestern Iberia by an oceanic route, all of them avoided the sea completely. Indeed, until the Vandals took over North Africa and the Visigoths did the same in Spain, the barbarians were carefully kept away from Mediterranean shores by Roman authorities.

The care shown by the Romans did not mean that the Roman Empire possessed any effective naval forces of its own in either the Mediterranean or northern Europe during these invasion years. Quite the contrary. It simply means that the Goths, Burgundians, Alemanni, and Franks were not maritime peoples and thus had no maritime skills to employ as yet. Certainly the Romans did not want them to overrun maritime communities where they could acquire those skills.

The history of the Vandals provides an example. Soon after arriving as conquerors in North Africa, the Vandals, although they were few in number, made Carthage their capital and took to the sea as pirates. It is hard not to see this action as one in which these Germans simply made use of preexisting shipping long based in African ports to send grain and olive oil to provision the city of Rome. At any rate, the Vandals were able to make use of sufficient naval resources to maintain a fleet, which they used to occupy ports in the Balearics, Sardinia, and Corsica and to raid the Italian mainland, including an attack which Gaiseric, their king, made on the city of Rome in 455.

We know little concerning the way the Vandals organized their naval contingents except that they are always referred to as pirates by Roman authorities, which suggests that their fleets were essentially irregular forces similar to those we find organized along the same coast later on by the Muslims. When Justinian attacked them during the sixth century, we are told he managed to lure their entire fleet of 120 ships away from Carthage by encouraging revolts in the Vandals' island empire, so he could land on Tunisian shores unopposed. The reference to a Vandal fleet implies that by this time they had a small standing navy based upon the dockyards and arsenal which Carthage had long possessed and supplied with timber for naval construction from nearby western North African shores. Most studies have overestimated the importance of Vandal sea power—some even going so far as to suggest that they were able to cut connections by sea between the Latin west and the Greek east in the late fifth century. This is certainly an exaggeration. The Vandals never held the island of Sicily, and, though they were able to control grain and olive oil sources on which Rome relied by getting control of North Africa, they probably did more damage through their control of these resources than they did through raids on Italy or even on Rome itself. Since both Sicily and the Adriatic remained Roman or Ostrogothic throughout this period, the Vandals' role in controlling trade between east and west was minimal at best.

What Vandal naval power in these years exemplifies, then, is not so much its own strength as the disorganization or lack of organization upon the sea of Roman imperial opponents. These latter lacked any fleet capable of opposing Vandal flotillas, and the one attempt they made to organize one on an *ad hoc* basis in 472 during the reign of Emperor Leo of Constantinople failed due to the incompetence of the Roman naval command, as the following account of the destruction of the Roman fleet by Vandal flotillas makes very clear.

> But the Vandals . . . raised their sails [when they found the Roman fleet anchored in a bay without lookouts] and, taking in tow the boats which, . . . they had made ready with no men in them, they sailed against the enemy [the Romans]. And when they came near, they set fire to the boats which they were towing, when their sails were bellied by the wind, and let them go against the Roman fleet. And since there were a great number of ships there, these boats easily spread fire wherever they struck. . . . And as the fire advanced in this way the Roman fleet was filled with tumult, as was natural, and with a great din that rivalled the noise caused by the wind and the roaring of the flames, as the soldiers together with the sailors shouted orders to one another and pushed off with their poles the fire-boats and their own ships as well, which were being destroyed by one another in complete disorder. And already the Vandals too were at hand ramming and sinking the ships, and making booty [capturing] of such of the soldiers as attempted to escape, and of their arms as well. [Procopius, *History of the Wars*, III, 17–22, trans. H.B. Dewing (Cambridge, Mass., 1953, p. 61.]

If Vandal naval power ruled the waters west of Sicily, it was by default rather than because of any essential strength of its own. It played little role in the affairs of Spain, Italy, and southern Gaul during its period of greater power other than to speed the decay of the city of Rome—a decline which had been in progress for more than a century.

One must have similar reservations about barbarian sea power in Atlantic waters during this same fifth century. We now know that Roman naval defenses in the Atlantic were not able to survive long after the withdrawal of the Roman legions from Britain in 412 and that the waters of the Irish Sea, the English Channel, and the North Sea became a happy hunting ground of loosely organized Irish, Pictish, Saxon, and Jutish raiders. But one should not overestimate the power of these flotillas. Despite their activities in these waters down to the time of Clovis (466?–511), Roman local authorities were able to maintain authority over most of Gaul north of the Loire. Elsewhere, other leaders, led by the legendary Arthur, were able to limit barbarian penetration into the more civilized parts of Britain. During these same years tribesmen from western British shores were even able to move en masse across the channel and begin to transform Amoricum into Brittany. Even communication between Britain and the continent was never really severed.

What then was the nature of the sea power exercised by barbarian peoples along these shores during this period? It was probably quite similar to that which Viking Danes and Norwegians displayed several centuries later. The story of Hengist and Horsa, apocryphal though it may be, rests upon a kernel of truth, portraying as it does how several shiploads of pirate adventurers first agreed to serve a British prince for gold and then murdered him and attempted to take over his authority. It was only *after* such adventurers had managed to establish themselves on the shores of Britain that other bands of Jutes, Angles, and Saxons were able to cross the Channel and North Sea in sufficient numbers to begin that slow transformation of Britain into England. By 500, however, only the very first steps in such a process had been taken.

Let us now consider the changes in maritime technology that came about as a result of this fifth-century movement of barbarian peoples about the northern seas of Europe. Some of these peoples, who had had regular contact with the Roman world, which lay across narrow seas from them, had managed to develop considerable maritime skills of their own, or had copied such skills from their Roman opponents. Most Irish and Picts may have used skin curraughs—some of them capable of long Atlantic voyages—but they also possessed better wooden ships using sails, which explains why Roman coins of the late empire have been found in Iceland. So, too, did at least some Saxon raiders, according to Sidonius, who describes them as skillful navigators of ships with sails.

But the mass of those who followed in the wake of the leaders of the attack on Britain arrived in large numbers from across the Channel in primitive, open-oared craft like the Nydam ship, the Kvalsund boats, and the vessel discovered at Sutton Hoo. Perhaps the use of

Alexander the Great is shown descending to the sea bottom in an illustration from *Romance of Alexander*, ca 1340. He purportedly used a diving bell to make the observation that big fishes ate up the little ones, a lesson he applied in his adventures on land! Bodleian Library, MS. Bodley 264, f. 90.

such primitive craft is especially true of the Angles, who seem to have been a Baltic rather than a North Sea people before their movement to the southeast which ended up in Britain. Nevertheless, although many of our English ancestors were technologically backward in the maritime skills which the Romans of Gaul, Spain, and Britain had long possessed, such skills had not completely disappeared from the northern seas. Rather, by the year 500, they lingered on along shores formerly controlled by Rome and merged with skills possessed by the barbarian newcomers to form the new maritime and naval traditions that we will examine in subsequent chapters.

As the Roman world came to an end in northern France and Britain, it also finally disappeared in Italy as the Ostrogoths established themselves in this last Roman-ruled area of the western empire. This process really began in 476 when the last western emperor, Romulus Augustulus, was deposed by his barbarian *magister militum*, Odovacer. This event displeased the eastern emperor in Constantinople, who in 488 was eager to dispose of the barbarian Ostrogoths. They had settled just south of the Middle Danube and were raiding the eastern empire and menacing its Balkan provinces. To get rid of them and to punish Odovacer at the same time for his presumption in making himself the ruler of Italy, the emperor in the east sent Theodoric, the young king of the Ostrogoths, and his people west into Italy. By 490 Theodoric had succeeded in eliminating Odovacer and in establishing himself as king of Italy, Illyria, and a part of southern France, which he rescued from the Franks and Burgundians. By 500 this extraordinarily able barbarian king had completed the Germanic conquest of the western empire and had set up in Ravenna a kingdom which displayed barbarian-Roman collaboration at its best.

What happened when Theodoric's conquest of Italy ended whatever remained of the Roman naval organization, which Augustus had established after Actium half a millennium before, and which his successors had maintained in some form ever since in the Middle Sea? The answer is that one must now distinguish between maritime vigor and naval power. This presents us with a paradox, for by the last years of the fifth century we have considerable evidence that maritime trade was again flourishing, especially in eastern Mediterranean waters.

Using relatively small two-masted sailing ships known as *naves*, which are depicted in frescos from Ravenna, merchants from Syria, Egypt, and the Aegean-Black Sea area now took to sea in large numbers and carried cargoes of grain, timber, wine, and other provisions to thriving metropolises such as Constantinople, Antioch, and Alexandria. Some of them, called *Syri*, began to sail west to Italy, Spain, and southern France as well, where they revived the importance of Marseilles and settled in considerable numbers at Ravenna.

We now know that this maritime revival was probably marked by better methods of frame-first ship construction in Aegean waters and perhaps even in the Adriatic, where there were abundant supplies of available ship timber, and the people possessed the technical skills to use them. We also can see in the flourishing states of the eastern empire under the rule of Anastasius (491–518) or Ostrogothic Italy under Theodoric (493–526) or even in Visigothic Spain that the worst days of the fifth century were over, and a new era was at hand in the Middle and Black Sea areas. This was true even though the eastern

Roman world still had no naval forces of its own, and only the Vandals to the west possessed an organized navy. An age of weakness on the sea had ended, and a new one was about to begin in the Mediterranean.

Turning to the north, let us examine the situation which prevailed in the gray waters of the Atlantic and in the narrow seas which surrounded the British Isles about A.D. 500. Here considerable change also had begun to modify extensively the pattern which had prevailed in late Roman times. And here the contrast with the vigorous maritime trade of the Mediterranean, newly revived, is dramatic. Only a few Romanized inhabitants still huddled in the ports of the Saxon shore or those that faced the Severn. Not a single major port survived in Britain or along the Channel into the sixth century, although some were to revive again later on. The older Roman pattern seemed to have disappeared.

Instead, two new northern maritime centers began to emerge. These centers differed considerably from those found here earlier. One was a Celtic Atlantic thalassocracy (from the Greek for control of the seas) centering around the Irish Sea and Britanny and extending south to Coruna in Iberian Galicia and north to the Shetland and Orkney islands. How peaceful this thalassocracy was it is difficult to say, but we have no evidence for any great conflicts on the waters of the Atlantic, which were to be traversed in the next few centuries by numerous Irish saints and missionaries.

The second maritime area, much more tentative in form, surrounded the North Sea and much of the English Channel and included most of eastern England, Frisia, and northern Germany within its compass. It also at times extended into the Baltic and Scandinavian area. Later traditions reaching us through poems such as *Beowulf* and the evidence provided us by archeologists indicate that this area in its proto-Viking form was much more primitive in a maritime sense than that of the Celts to the west, though it was to the former that much of the future belonged.

So it was that as the ancient world of the Roman Empire came to an end, we can see a new series of maritime areas emerge about the northern seas of Europe and in the Mediterranean as well. These pages will attempt to trace the destinies of these areas in the medieval centuries to come.

Byzantine Naval Power and Shipping, 500–1291

IN 518 THE REIGN of the Emperor Anastasius came to an end in Constantinople, and he was succeeded by the bluff, soldierly Justin I. The real power, however, was exercised by his nephew, Justinian, who succeeded him as Emperor in 527 and ruled until 565. It is under the latter that a new naval era began in the Mediterranean.

In many ways Justinian turned out to be an able but typical emperor, who, by his interest in efficient administration, legal reform, diplomacy, religious leadership, and economic controls, followed the policies of his late Roman predecessors Constantine and Theodosius. In one respect, however, he was an innovator, because it was he who restored Roman naval power to the Mediterranean or, to be more exact, established a new eastern Roman or Byzantine navy, which was to continue to be a potent force in this part of the world until the time of the Fourth Crusade (1202–1204).

What seems to have impelled Justinian to act as an innovator in naval matters was his desire to reconquer the western Mediterranean world, which by 500 had, as we have noted, fallen into the hands of barbarian Vandal, Ostrogothic, and Visigothic monarchs, who controlled its shores and its islands as well. For this task he had available a full treasury left him by his predecessor Anastasius and an excellent professional army led by Belisarius and other talented generals, who had been battle-tested in border wars waged against the Persians. But if he was to reconquer the west, he needed something more—a navy—to transport his armies, to deal with Vandal fleets and pirates, and to assure his armed forces of sea communication between western battlefronts in North Africa, Italy, and beyond, and in the eastern Mediterranean.

Soon after his accession to power he began to build a large fleet in eastern Roman ports. Procopius, who knew this fleet first hand, describes it as follows:

> And for the whole force five hundred ships were required, no one of which was able to carry more than fifty thousand *Medimni* [about one and a half bushels], nor any one less than three thousand. And in all the vessels together there were thirty thousand sailors, Egyptians and Ionians for the most part and Cilicians, and one commander was appointed over all the ships, Calonymus of Alexandria. And they had also ships of war prepared as for sea-fighting, to the number of ninety-two, and they were single-banked ships covered by decks, in order that the men rowing them might if possible not be exposed to the bolts of the enemy. Such boats are called "dromones" (runners) by those of the present time; for they are able to attain a great speed. In these sailed two thousand men of Byzantium, who were all rowers as well as fighting men; for there was not a single superfluous man among them. [Procopius, *History of the Wars*, III, xi, 13–16, trans. H.B. Dewing (Cambridge, Mass., 1953), pp. 105–107.]

We know little more concerning the size of this fleet or the exact nature of its vessels, except that it was built in a number of dockyards in Alexandria, along the Syrian coast, and in the north Aegean Sea or at Constantinople. Since the Vandal fleet was a possible opponent, we know a number of warships were included in it, as well as sufficient transports to carry a relatively large expeditionary force, including cavalry. These warships, however, were never destined to see action at sea, since the Vandal fleet was lured away from its North African bases by Justinian's diplomacy, and before the ruse was discovered, General Belisarius had landed his forces unopposed and had destroyed the Vandal kingdom in a single battle outside Carthage. Following this victory, the Vandal Empire and its fleet fell like a ripe plum into Byzantine hands.

With the threat of Vandal naval power removed, Belisarius proceeded swiftly to seize Sicily and then landed in southern Italy. From there he advanced northward to take Rome and Ravenna. Despite his command of the sea, however, he began to run into trouble, and his campaign bogged down. There were a number of reasons for his failure. First, Persians in the east opened a second front, tying up troops, which could not now be spared to send to Italy. Second, bubonic plague from the east reached the Mediterranean world and carried off a large part of the population, upon which the empire depended for soldiers. And third, Justinian deliberately reduced the number of reinforcements he sent Belisarius because he feared that too much success would allow his general a popularity which might encourage Belisarius to make an effort to replace him on the throne. Finally, the inhabitants of the reconquered areas of North Africa and Italy found Justinian's tax gatherers, who arrived in the wake of his armies, unbearable and rose in revolt against them. Belisarius's stalled offensive began to turn into a slow retreat southward as the Ostrogoths found a new leader of ability in the person of King Totila. Rome and much of southern Italy fell into barbarian hands again.

The final blow was the decision by the Ostrogoths to build a fleet of their own to challenge the new eastern Roman fleet on the sea. When this happened, Belisarius was recalled as commander, and it looked as if more than a decade of war in Italy was to come to an end without any lasting result. At this point Justinian made a last supreme effort. He organized a new army, entrusting it to the aged eunuch Narses, who could not threaten his rule by founding a dynasty of his own, and sent him *by land* into Italy. Narses proved to be an able commander and in one battle utterly destroyed the Ostrogothic army. All resistance collapsed, and a battered Italy, devastated by fifteen years of war, was at last Justinian's. As Italy became Roman again, a naval flotilla sailed west to regain Andalusia and southern Spain and Moroccan territory just across from Gibraltar for Justinian as well. By 550, most of the western Mediterranean, including Italy, North Africa, southern Spain, and the Balearic Islands, Corsica, and Sardinia were Roman again, and Justinian's fleets and the commercial shipping of his empire could sail through the Mediterranean and Black seas unopposed from east to west.

A Byzantine lateen-rigged ship represented in a Greek manuscript of ca 880. The earliest representation of a lateen sail is from the second century. By the ninth century it was the preferred sail in the Mediterranean. Bibliothèque Nationale MS. Parisinus Graecus 510, f. 3.

How should we judge this revived *Romania* and the new naval power which had helped to make it possible? It has been much misunderstood by historians. They have pointed out that soon after Justinian died, Slavs overran much of the interior of the Balkans as far south as southern Greece and that Lombards did the same in the interior of Italy. Therefore, they conclude, Justinian's reconquest of the west was a mistake, which sapped the basic strength of the empire and made the later loss of its fairest eastern provinces inevitable.

These historians have failed to understand that what Justinian created and what was maintained by his successors down to the last years of Heraclius some eight decades later was essentially a naval empire. Justinian's empire was more like the empire of eighteenth- and nineteenth-century Britain than it was like the earlier Roman Empire from which it had sprung. Sea power held it together, and not the legions or network of roads upon which Augustus, Diocletian, and Constantine had depended. Armies were, of course, necessary to defend dangerous Armenian–North Syrian frontiers from Persian attacks. But elsewhere, wherever possible, expensive professional mercenary cavalry and infantry forces were used as sparingly as possible, their place being taken by extensive fortifications, an active diplomacy, a militia system, economic pressures upon potential enemies, and even subsidies to allies like the Franks or the Ghassanid Arab rulers of the Syrian borderlands. The indispensable cement was a naval power which could be shifted from one part of the Mediterranean–Black Sea world to another and carry armed forces to threatened areas. Thus Britain used her command of the sea during her second hundred years war with France from 1689 to 1815, and later on as well, a policy noted by Admiral Mahan in the late nineteenth century and discussed in his famous works on the influence of sea power upon history.

How was this naval power, so essential to this restored Roman Empire, organized? We cannot be absolutely sure, though our sources provide us with some indication of its use. It seems clear that, since the emperors of Constantinople had no naval opponents in the Middle Sea or in the Euxine, which they dominated, they did not need to build large warships. Instead, they could concentrate on smaller, swift, oared vessels as their principal attack arm—ancestors of the later fast *dromons* and galleys which were to feature subsequent periods on the sea. They also must have needed to have some more cumbersome supply ships, which were undoubtedly built like those two-masted *naves* we mentioned in our last chapter.

Constantinople, with its imperial arsenal and neighboring dockyards, was the empire's chief naval base, as is revealed by the large and effective fleets it could muster in the 620s under Emperor Heraclius, when it beat off attacks by the migrant Avars from the Danube basin. Other smaller bases existed at Alexandria and along the Syrian shore, where, in the seventh century, the conquering Arabs were able to swiftly build ships and find crews for them to challenge Constantinople's naval mastery of the eastern Mediterranean. The small naval flotilla located at Alexandria probably had as one of its main duties the convoying of grain ships on their annual voyage to provision the capital to the north. Another small naval force was maintained at Cherson to protect Byzantine interests and trade along the northern shores of the Black Sea.

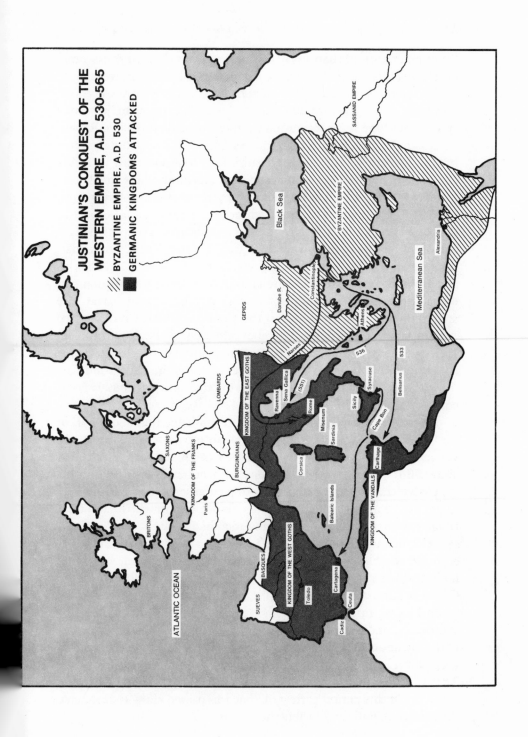

JUSTINIAN'S CONQUEST OF THE
WESTERN EMPIRE, A.D. 530-565

▨ BYZANTINE EMPIRE, A.D. 530
■ GERMANIC KINGDOMS ATTACKED

ATLANTIC OCEAN

BRITONS

SAXONS

KINGDOM OF THE FRANKS

BURGUNDIANS

LOMBARDS

GEPIDS

Danube R.

Black Sea

BYZANTINE EMPIRE

SASSANID EMPIRE

Constantinople

Athens

Narses

(551)

KINGDOM OF THE EAST GOTHS

Ravenna

Sena Gallica

Rome

536

Misenum

Sardinia

Corsica

Sicily

Syracuse

Balearic Islands

Cape Bon

Belisarius

533

Carthage

KINGDOM OF THE VANDALS

Mediterranean Sea

Alexandria

Paris

SUEVES

BASQUES

KINGDOM OF THE WEST GOTHS

Toledo

Cartagena

Cadiz

Ceuta

More important than any of these eastern naval contingents, however, except for the main fleet located in the Golden Horn, were those
in the west. Here, where governors had control of both the civil administration and the armed forces, there were three principal naval
commands. One was centered on the old Roman naval base of Ravenna under the direct control of the exarch, who governed Italy as an
imperial viceroy, with a possible subsidiary base and a few warships
at Naples or Syracuse. A second and even more important naval command was that which was exercised by the exarch of Africa from
Carthage—the main western Mediterranean commercial center of
the period. Its principal duty was to protect the regular export of grain
and olive oil—probably to western Italian ports. The Carthaginian
warships formed a large enough naval force to allow Heraclius to
assemble a fleet there with which he could sail to Constantinople in
610 and overthrow the Emperor Phocas. A final western naval base
and command was exercised by the Count or Duke who governed
Andalusia and the Strait of Gibraltar and so held the key to the entrance to the Atlantic. Probably the last commander of this fleet was
the famous Count Julian who furnished the Muslims, Musa and Tar-
ik, with the ships that allowed them to cross into Spain in 711 and
conquer it for Islam.

Judging from later evidence, it seems probable that about half of
the imperial fleet was stationed in Constantinople, while the rest was
scattered throughout the Mediterranean and Black seas as outlined
above. But what gave this system its peculiar flexibility and inexpensive character was its ability to regularly supplement the contingents of warships and supply vessels which formed the imperial
naval establishment by impressing merchant vessels into imperial
service when needed—in a manner similar to medieval England's later *prise of ships* or the *themal* navies of subsequent Byzantine
history. Such a system, especially in maritime centers like Ravenna,
Carthage, Constantinople, or Alexandria, allowed large fleets to be
assembled at minimum expense. Such fleets assembled in Constantinople and elsewhere allowed Heraclius to maintain his armies
in the distant Caucasus during his long wars with the Persians and to
keep control of western provinces in faraway Spain, Italy, and North
Africa at the same time. In many ways it was this system, which the
emperors of this period perfected, that was passed along to influence
the maritime policies of their successors.

Divers at work on the wreck of the Serçe Liman ship off the Turkish coast. Note the labels and the use of grids to identify areas of
the wreck. Institute of Nautical Archaeology, Texas A & M University. Photo by Donald Frey.

Abruptly, as the reign of the aged hero Heraclius ended in 641, a new era, which was to affect Byzantium's navy and its performance in a vital way, began in the Mediterranean. This new era was ushered in, of course, by the surge of Arab-Muslim forces emerging from their desert homes in Arabia to conquer Syria, Egypt, Libya, and the Persian Empire. Byzantium woke up to find that her elaborate system of fortifications, subsidies, and sea power could not protect her richest eastern provinces, partially disaffected by their dislike of the empire's fiscal impositions and religious policies.

Not only was Byzantium unable to use her navy effectively to prevent the loss of Syria and Egypt to the Arabs—her only naval action of significance being a brief reoccupation of Alexandria which ended in failure when her forces were expelled in 645—but worse was to follow. For almost immediately Muslim conquests were followed by Arabs taking to the sea, using the ships and crews available in Syrian and Egyptian ports. The new fleet's first action was the seizure of Cyprus in 651. It was followed up by a series of raids on shores which remained loyal to Constantinople as far west as Sicily. These actions culminated in 655 in a great Byzantine naval defeat in a bay off the coast of Asia Minor called "The Battle of the Masts." It has been said that this defeat, in which Arab tactics consisted of grappling with enemy ships, cutting their rigging and sails, and rendering them helpless, almost resulted in the capture of the young Byzantine emperor Constans II, who only escaped with great difficulty. By 655, then, Byzantium had not only lost its fairest oriental provinces, but also faced a new and formidable rival in a Mediterranean world which it had dominated for the past century.

Fortunately for Constans II, the Muslims were not able to follow up their naval victory at the Battle of the Masts because in 656 their Caliph, Othman, was assassinated in Mecca, and his successors, the Caliphs Ali and Muawiyah, began a long rivalry ending in civil war. Not until almost a decade had passed was the latter able to secure his position as caliph and set up his Ummayad family as hereditary rulers in their new capital of Damascus. Until then, the Arabs were unable to return to the offensive on the sea against those provinces that remained loyal to Constantinople.

Constans II and his son and successor, Constantine IV, made good use of this lull in their conflict with the Arabs. The former sailed with an army to the west, where he was able to strengthen Byzantium's military and naval defenses in Italy, North Africa, and Sicily. Of particular importance were his checking of the tendency of the exarchs in the west to make themselves independent of Constantinople, and his limiting Lombard advances in Italy.

Even more important, he and his son established a new naval system as part of an overall change in the empire's defensive strategy—one which was to serve Byzantium well and become the cornerstone of its resistance to land and sea assaults. A small professional imperial navy armed with Greek fire was stationed near the capital, where it had available to it all the support this great city could provide. Two large army contingents, also composed of professional troops and located in the city, supplemented these naval forces.

The use of Greek fire deserves a special mention here because it served Byzantium well as a special secret weapon. Made of a combustible mixture of phosphorus and saltpeter which could be "fired" from a tube onto enemy vessels to set them afire, Greek fire was a terrifying incendiary device available only to the Byzantines. Its unnatural properties included the ability to burn in water. The Arabs were greatly impressed by this weapon and had to adjust their tactics to avoid these early flamethrowers, which could turn wooden ships into floating infernos.

In those Anatolian provinces which were far from the capital and exposed to direct Arab assaults, we now find military governors or *strategoi* appointed who combined a command of all the armed forces in their provinces or *themes*, as they were called, with control of the civil administration, just as the emperor himself did in Constantinople. This system was not completely new, since such *strategoi* were in a sense simply copies of the western exarchs, who had exercised similar authority since the time of Justinian. Some scholars also believe that they assumed such powers very gradually, beginning as early as the Persian invasions during Heraclius's reign.

A somewhat new development, however, was the organizing of local militia forces to defend each province from Arab or other outside attacks. By the mid-seventh century small landholders were guaranteed an unalienable freehold right to their property in return for regular military service when called up by their *strategoi*. Thus, the empire's remaining provinces were provided with a double defense system which the straitened finances of the hard-pressed empire could afford—a militia system near its borders backed up by a professional military force in the capital city of Constantinople.

This system was easily adapted to naval defense. Already in Italy

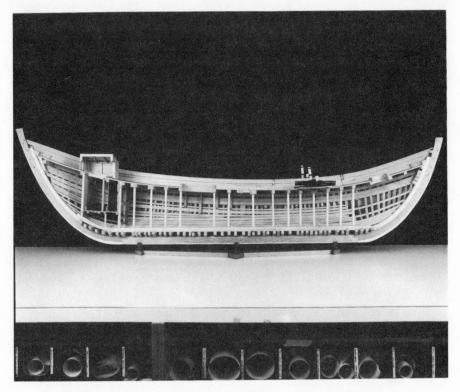

Half model of the seventh-century Byzantine ship excavated at
Yassi Ada near Bodrum, Turkey. J. Richard Steffy, Institute of Nautical Archaeology, Texas A & M University. Photo by Bobbe Baker.

and North Africa local naval forces had long been placed under the
control of the exarchs, who were similar to eastern *strategoi*. Now in
the east a special large naval theme was created which included the
south coast of Asia Minor and the islands of the Aegean and whose
governor was an admiral. Those whose ships and ship service were
mustered for war by this admiral were rewarded with freehold ten-
ures on the same terms as the soldier militia of the military themes.

How well did this system work in defending the empire from naval attack? Very well indeed. For instance, it helped the empire survive
a great Arab assault, which penetrated the sea of Marmora and block-
aded Constantinople itself between 672 and 678 only to be driven back

to Syrian and Egyptian bases with a great loss of ships. Theophanes, the Byzantine historian, writing somewhat later on describes this Arab attack as follows:

> In this year [673] the deniers of Christ [the Arabs] readied a great expedition. They sailed to and wintered in Kilikia [Cilicia]. . . . When Constantine [IV] learned of the movement . . . he prepared huge two-storied warships equipped with Greek fire and siphon-carrying warships. . . .
>
> All day long from dawn to dusk there was combat . . . [near the walls of Constantinople]. The Arabs retreated to Kyzikos [Cyzius, across the Sea of Marmora], to winter there. In the spring they set out in the same way to meet the Christians in sea-battle. They did the same thing for seven years, but with the aid of God and His Mother they were disgraced. . . . They retreated in great distress. . . . As their expedition was going away after God had ruined it, it was overtaken by a tempestuous winter storm. . . . It was shivered to atoms and completely destroyed. . . .
>
> At that time Kallinikos, an artificer from Heliopolis, fled to the Romans. He had devised a sea fire which ignited the Arab ships and burned them with all hands. Thus it was that the Romans returned with victory and discovered the sea fire. [*The Chronicle of Theophanes*, trans. H. Turtledove (Philadelphia, 1982), pp. 52–53.]

At about the same time, the new system also seems to have allowed the Exarchate of Africa to hold its own against an invading Arab army. After these victories, it seems to have made possible retaliatory raids by Byzantine maritime forces against Syrian shores—raids supported by native Lebanese-Christian forces known as Mardaites, which only ended with a payment of tribute to Constantinople by the Ummayad Caliphate.

A few years later, Byzantium faced an even greater threat, when the first erratic reign of the emperor Justinian II (685–695) and his vengeful return to power (705–711) dangerously weakened the empire's military and naval defenses. As a result, the Arabs were able to conquer Byzantine Tunisia in 696 and then expand westward ending with the conquest of Visigothic Spain in 711. Thus, by the end of the second reign of Justinian II, the Arabs had at last managed to break through the Byzantine naval defenses of the central Mediterranean and gain for themselves in North Africa a new potential center of naval strength.

Emboldened by these victories, the Caliph Walid mustered a great fleet to attack Constantinople a second time. It consisted of North African, Syrian, and Egyptian naval contingents and army units as well. The fleet sailed north in the summer of 717 and by the winter of 718 the city was under siege. Fortunately, the empire's new ruler, Leo III, the Isaurian, proved an able commander. He persuaded the Bulgars to attack the Arab invaders from the land. Then, after an especially cold winter had demoralized the besiegers, he sailed out of the Golden Horn with his small but effective navy, armed with Greek fire as had been the case in 678, and shattered the Muslim naval armada. The remaining Muslims were driven out of the Aegean with such great losses that only a handful of vessels made it back to home ports. Theophanes again is our source of information on the expedition, and he writes as follows:

On September 1 . . . Suleiman [the overall Arab commander] and his emirs arrived with their expedition. He had front-line ships, fighting merchantmen, and warships; their number was 1,800. . . . After two days the south wind began to blow; they left that area and sailed past the city. . . .

The Arabs' great ships were useless because they were weighed down by their cargo; and so they left behind about twenty merchantmen to guard their backs. . . . Good weather came while they were in the Bosporos . . . so Maslama [the Arab admiral] pushed his ships farther forward. With God's help, the pious Emperor [Leo III] immediately sent [Greek-] fire ships against them from the citadel which turned them into blazing wrecks. Some of them, still burning, smashed into the sea wall. . . . Because of this the spirits of the city's inhabitants were lifted, but their foes shivered in terror, recognizing how strong the liquid fire was. . . .

When it was Spring, Sufyan arrived with an expedition organized in Egypt; he had four hundred food-carrying merchantmen and warships. When he learned of the power of Greek fire, he bypassed Bithynia . . . [later] crossing over to the other shore (across from the city). . . . Yezid soon arrived with another expedition, which had been formed in Africa. He had two hundred sixty merchantmen, with both arms and supplies. Like Sufyan, he had learned about the liquid fire. He anchored . . . far away [from the city]. . . .

The Emperor learned . . . of the two fleets hidden in the bay. He readied fire-carrying siphons and put them aboard warships and two-storied ships, then dispatched them against the two

fleets. Thanks to the cooperation of God through His wholly im-
maculate Mother's intercession, the enemy was sunk on the
spot. Seizing booty and the Arab's supplies, our men returned
with joy and victory. [*The Chronicle of Theophanes*, trans. H.
Turtledove (Philadelphia, 1982), pp. 88–89.]

Soon thereafter, a great land victory cleared the Arab invaders out of
Asia Minor. The empire had been saved in no small measure by its
naval forces.

Unfortunately, Leo decided to follow up his naval victory by
meddling in religious matters, and he espoused a religious reform
movement called Iconoclasm, which was very unpopular in Italy and
in those parts of the Aegean where themal fleets were located. The
Pope and the inhabitants of Rome and Ravenna refused to accept
Leo's Iconoclastic reforms and themal fleets nearer home staged a
serious revolt. Under Constantine V (744–775), Leo's son, Byzantium
advanced again on the sea, when in 747 the Byzantine fleet caught the
Muslim fleet of Syria and Egypt in a bay off the island of Cyprus and
annihilated it. The victory was followed up by the elimination of the
Arab North African contingents, which for some decades had been
raiding Sicily with impunity. By 750 the Muslim naval threat to the
empire had been eliminated. To make sure that it did not recur, Constantine V seems to have completed a program begun by Justinian II
half a century earlier which denied Muslim merchants access to the
empire's markets except under strict controls—a policy which, when
it was enforced by Byzantium's naval flotillas, paralyzed Islamic
maritime strength in Syria, Egypt, and North Africa, and so struck at
the heart of its naval forces.

As had happened with Syria and Egypt a century earlier, however,
Byzantine sea power alone proved powerless to protect or retain a rich
and distant province which had become religiously disaffected, Italy.
Although Byzantium maintained a naval foothold in Venice near
Ravenna and kept control of Naples and parts of southern Italy—
none of which either the Carolingian Franks or the North African
Muslims were able to threaten seriously at this time, these losses of
territory in the long run were to be extremely important.

As it turned out, this brief control of the waters of the central and
eastern Mediterranean through a naval system begun by the Heraclians and perfected by the Isaurians was not destined to last more
than a few decades. By the first years of the ninth century, it ceased to

function effectively, as the weak rule of the Empress Irene and her immediate successors, social discontent among the lower classes, and a renewal of Iconoclasm culminated in the revolt of Thomas the Slav in 823–825. In this revolt the themal fleets of the Aegean were destroyed, and those of Sicily, led by a certain Admiral Eugenius, went over to the Muslims. Suddenly much of the naval strength upon which Byzantium depended to maintain control of the waters of the Middle Sea had disappeared. A new age was at hand.

Almost at once the Muslim world, which for eighty years had been quiescent upon the sea, returned to the offensive and began to reverse the results of the earlier duel with Byzantium. Cyprus again came under the control of Muslim naval forces based in Syria and Cilicia; Crete in 826 or 827 was seized by Islamic Spanish adventurers who had just been driven from Alexandria; and Sicily was invaded by North African Muslims, who took Palermo and began a slow but steady conquest of the island. Even the Spanish Muslims in the far west added the Balearics to their realm.

Byzantium, especially after the resolution of the Iconoclast controversy in 843, made an effort to resist, with some success. Smaller naval themes were set up near the entrance to the Aegean and along the south shores of Asia Minor to resist the pirate flotillas of Crete and Cyprus, though neither island was recovered from the occupation by the Muslims. Though Sicily was finally completely lost to the Muslims in 902, along with Corsica and Sardinia, advance Islamic pirate bases around Bari and Monte Garigliano in southern Italy were eventually eliminated. Southern Italy's heel and toe (Calabria and Apulia), Venice, and the Adriatic remained under Byzantium's naval control. And so did the Black Sea area, where Russian attacks on Constantinople were defeated in 860 and 907, and trade agreements with the rulers of Kiev were negotiated in 911 and 942. Byzantium, badly battered on the sea by the first half of the tenth century, still remained a naval power of some importance.

Finally, however, the naval picture began to change in the early tenth century. An able co-emperor, Romanus Lecapenus, who had served as admiral of the fleet, began a period of naval reorganization. He built new large *dromons* or warships and changed naval tactics from the defensive posture advocated by Emperor Leo VI in his *Tactikon* to a new aggressive stance in line with that advocated by the military aristocracy. By 963 the fleet, led by Emperor Nicephorus

Phocas, was able to recapture Crete using an estimated 3,000 vessels in its armada and amphibious tactics, which saw special ships land on the beach and discharge heavily armored cavalry directly on the sand. Two years later Cyprus was retaken, and nearby Cilicia and northern Syria as well, the latter along with its great city of Antioch being captured in a campaign in which army and navy worked closely together. A few years later in 972, the navy was employed to help defeat Prince Sviatoslav of Kiev on the lower Danube and help Emperor John Zimisces break the power of the First Bulgarian Empire. An aggressive new Byzantine fleet had appeared in the waters of the eastern Mediterranean and the Black Sea.

This fleet was much less effectively used during the reign of Basil II (985–1025), the greatest emperor of the Macedonian line, who concentrated most of his attention upon land campaigns to destroy what remained of the Bulgarian Empire and to advance his frontiers into Armenia. Nevertheless, it did help to assure Byzantium a firm control over southern Italy and considerable influence over both the papacy and Venice as long as Basil lived.

Basil II died before he was able to complete his grand design in the west to use the fleet to retake Sicily from the Muslims. Though his unworthy successors finally made an effort to do so between 1038 and 1043, they lacked his political acumen and abandoned their commander, George Maniaces, before the island's conquest had been completed. Something of the strength of Byzantium's great fleets of the tenth century, however, remained down to the end of the Macedonian dynasty in 1056. As a result its flotillas maintained a mastery of the waters near imperial shores unmatched since the days of Leo III and Constantine V in the eighth century.

It might be wise at this point to pause and examine certain aspects of the tactics, technology, and strategic considerations which characterized Byzantine naval forces in late Macedonian times when the empire was at the height of its power. This navy was quite different from what it had been earlier, since it was now essentially an offensive force, composed of a number of large, oared *dromons*, swift, scouting, oared galleys, and two- or three-masted sailing *naves* and transport ships of various sorts—supplemented in time of war by merchant vessels pressed into service, as of yore. The imperial fleet still used Greek fire, but, since Byzantium's naval opponents were by now well acquainted with its use, it had lost its element of surprise.

Instead, the newest weapons used afloat were various kinds of catapults adapted for use at sea from experience in land siege warfare. Such weapons were used against a Russian fleet in the Propontis with great effect.

Since the navy was conceived of as an offensive arm, there was less need for provincial or themal naval fleets constructed primarily for defensive purposes. They were not part of the attack force which the dominant military landowning aristocrats were leading abroad on military campaigns. As a result, themal fleets lost their importance and, by the end of Basil II's reign, had all but disappeared. Only Venice and Amalfi in the west had vessels which could at times be used to support the ships of an imperial navy, which was generally stationed near Constantinople.

During the tenth and eleventh centuries, the way in which the empire organized the economy also had an important effect upon its naval forces. Since Isaurian times the government had run the empire as a fortress, economically speaking, forbidding its merchants to export its gold currency or trade abroad, and confining foreign merchants to certain special trade portals so that imports and exports could be carefully controlled. This restrictive policy may have strengthened the empire in time of war by denying to the Muslim maritime world, in particular, the timber and arms it could not procure along its own shores, and so weakening its efforts on the sea. But it had important effects upon the empire's own merchant shipping and merchant class in general. In its Black Sea and Aegean heartlands, where Byzantium was able to enforce its control, the policy tended to limit the prosperity of its native traders, who anyway preferred for social reasons to invest their commercial profits in land, rather than in new trading ventures. By the tenth century, if not earlier, Byzantine merchants more and more resembled those of American antebellum Charleston or New Orleans, who similarly invested their capital in land and not in further trade.

This practice divorced Byzantine naval power from commercial enterprise. Consequently, the empire's main fleets at Constantinople were government-built and operated, while its declining provincial flotillas were relegated to an economic world of cabotage, or small-scale coastal and interisland transactions. Such a world invited its foreign commerce to be the preserve of Russians, Italians, or other outsiders, who were not subject to the same internal governmental imperatives.

There were, however, by the tenth and eleventh centuries certain exceptions to this state of affairs which need comment: namely the merchants and sailors of Venice and of the Naples-Amalfi area of Italy, who were nominally part of the empire but who were too far away from Constantinople to be controlled. They were able to evade imperial regulations and trade freely with Muslim and Latin European ports, while still sending their ships regularly to Constantinople itself. Thus, by 1056 Byzantium had, through its own economic policies, created naval power and commercial strength in cities such as Venice and Amalfi which were to be a serious problem in the future. In these outlying cities, naval and commercial maritime strength were not divorced from one another as had happened in the heartland of the empire, but were clearly joined together to form naval forces which would, in the long run, seriously threaten Byzantium's control of the sea.

As the Macedonian line of rulers came to an end, the Byzantine Empire entered another half century of troubles, which affected its naval organization profoundly. Already during the reigns of Zoe and Theodora (1028–1056) control of the central government had fallen into the hands of a group of civil aristocrats who neglected the armed services, looted the treasury, and allowed the smallholders in the themes to disappear. Though two emperors of the military aristocratic group briefly held power after 1056, they were unable to reverse these trends. As a result, the army was disastrously defeated by the Seljuk Turks at Manzikert in 1071, and nothing was done to keep Byzantium's possessions in southern Italy from falling into the hands of Norman adventurers. These latter, whom we know as Robert and Roger Guiscard, were able to capitalize on Byzantium's weakness and establish a new realm, which has gone down in history as The Kingdom of Two Sicilies. By the time an able military aristocrat, Alexius Comnenus, became emperor in 1081, Byzantium had lost most of Anatolia to the Turks, all of southern Italy to the Normans, and was on the defensive on the Danube. It had only a few mercenaries available to protect it on the land, and it was defenseless at sea, for neither its imperial navy nor its provincial fleets were any longer in operation. That naval power which had been the backbone of Byzantine armed strength since the time of Justinian had ceased to exist.

Alexius Comnenus proved himself to be a ruler of great ability. Almost at once he enlisted the help of the Venetians to check Nor-

Noah's ark from an Old English poem on Genesis, ca
1000. The illustrator put on board so many animals and
people that he apparently felt it necessary to expand the
basic Viking or Norman dragon-ship into a high-rise
cruise vessel. By permission of the Bodleian Library, Oxford, MS. Junius 11, f. 66.

man attacks on imperial shores across the Strait of Otranto, paying
off Venice for her assistance by issuing a Golden Bull, which gave her
merchants special trading privileges in Constantinople and along the
Mediterranean shores of his empire. Alexius's daughter, Anna Comnena, has left us an account of the naval warfare between the Byzan-
tine-Venetian force and the Normans off the Albanian coast as follows:

When he [Robert Guiscard, the Norman commander] heard of Palaeologus' [the Byzantine commander] arrival in Dyrrachium [Durazzo], he at once had turrets constructed on his larger vessels, built of wood and covered with hides. And he speedily had everything necessary for a siege packed on board the ships, and horses and fully-equipped cavalry he embarked on the crusiers. . . . His plan was to surround Dyrrachium, when he reached it, with battering engines both on the land- and on the sea-side so as to strike dismay into the hearts of the inhabitants and also by thus hemming them in completely to take the town by assault. . . . When Robert had everything completed to his liking, he loosed anchor; the freightships, the triremes, the monoremes were drawn up in the battle array of nautical tradition, and thus in good order he started on his voyage.

The [Venetian] admirals though . . . gained a brilliant victory over him. . . . [Later on, Robert] recovering his spirits again attacked the Venetians. These were panic-stricken by his unexpected arrival; they at once bound together their larger vessels with ropes in the neighborhood of the harbour of Corfu, and having thus constructed what is called an "open sea-harbour" they drove the smaller vessels into it . . . then armed and awaited his [Robert's] coming. When he came, the battle began. . . . The Venetians had previously consumed all their provisions and consequently the boats were empty but for the soldiers; so the boats . . . floated about as if upheld by the surface of the water. . . . [During the battle] the soldiers rushed in a mass to the side of the ships facing the foe, and so were drowned; they numbered about thirteen thousand. The other ships were taken, crews and all. [*The Alexiad of the Princess Anna Comnena* (London, 1928; reprinted New York, 1978), pp. 95–6 and 145–46.]

The emperor followed up this victory with military campaigns along the lower Danube to secure the frontier. In the middle of the 1090s he turned to the Latin west and asked the Pope's help in procuring some western knights to aid him by clearing the Seljuk Turks from Asia Minor.

To his consternation, his plea for help resulted in the great movement to the Holy Land of Latin westerners which we call the First Crusade. But even before the Crusaders arrived in Constantinople, Alexius had begun to rebuild the Byzantine fleet. With this fleet he was able to regain control of the coastal areas of Asia Minor, restore Crete and Cyprus as naval bases, and keep Pisan and Genoese fleets from plundering the Aegean on their way to the Holy Land. Though he continued throughout his reign to strengthen his imperial fleets through a continuous rebuilding program, he was unable to reconstitute the themal fleets in the Aegean or change the passive nature of the empire's foreign trade. Instead, the Venetians made the most of the privileges granted them by the Golden Bull of 1086 and increased their share of the commerce of Constantinople and of the Aegean parts of *Romania* (the Eastern Roman Empire).

During the reign of John, who succeeded his father Alexius in 1118, naval policies changed very little. John maintained an effective imperial fleet in Constantinople and control of the strategic island bases of Crete and Cyprus, and even intervened with some success in Cilicia and Norman-controlled Antioch. His attempt to revoke his father's Golden Bull and to ally with the Pisans, however, backfired. The Venetians forced him to renew the Golden Bull with even more extensive privileges, and the Pisans began to play an important commercial role in Constantinople, which further emphasized the empire's passivity.

The rule of the third emperor of the Comneni house, Manuel, was even more important from a naval perspective. When Manuel became emperor, he faced two serious threats—forces of the Second Crusade, which descended on his empire on their way to the Holy Land, and a full-scale Norman attack by sea, led by the ambitious Roger II, the King of the Two Sicilies. He had to deal with both at the same time. Diplomacy was employed to push the crusading forces into the heart of Asia Minor, where they were badly defeated by the Turks and where some survivors who retreated to the coast were then ferried on to the Holy Land by Byzantine ships.

The more dangerous Norman forces of King Roger were attacked by a new imperial fleet built largely near Constantinople and by flotillas of Venice, which had allied with Manuel in return for a renewal of Venetian trading privileges. Eventually these forces were able to drive the Normans from Corfu and other parts of Greece, which they had occupied, and to restore the situation to what it had been earlier.

Manuel then decided to strengthen his naval forces, and he began a program of rebuilding which was to continue throughout his reign of more than three decades. He took the offensive in 1152 in Adriatic waters, reestablishing control over the Dalmatian coast, landing an expeditionary force in southern Italy, and allying himself with Ancona as a possible western entrepôt and competitor with Venice. In these efforts he was only partly successful. Venice turned against him and joined the Normans and the new German emperor, Frederick I, in driving his forces out of southern Italy. Although he kept control of Illyria, maintained his alliance with Ancona, and gave special privileges to the Genoese and Pisans, Manuel found he was forced to extend Venice's special trading privileges to encompass all of his empire south of the Black Sea.

From a naval point of view he was more successful elsewhere. He was able to make use of naval contingents along the Danube to assert a Byzantine hegemony over Hungary. He completely dominated Black Sea shores leading to Kievan Russia and Georgia. And he was able to employ his naval strength to help him conclude an alliance with the Latin kings of Jerusalem. He even raided Muslim Egypt from the sea. Finally, in 1171 he took revenge upon Venice by suddenly, without warning, seizing every Venetian ship trading with his empire—some 3,000 vessels in all, according to our sources. By the end of his reign, he had made Byzantine sea power an immensely powerful force in the entire eastern Mediterranean-Black Sea area and had shown himself to be the most successful naval-minded emperor since Nicephorus Phocas.

Careful examination of Manuel's sea power, however, reveals that it had serious limitations. It consisted almost entirely of imperial fleets built and based near Constantinople. Provincial fleets were not reconstituted, which meant that local areas such as Greece and the Aegean parts of the Eastern Roman Empire had no local maritime defenses of their own. Although he was able to strike a heavy blow against Venice's maritime and commercial exploitation of his empire by confiscating their merchant fleet in 1171, he simply replaced these privileged foreigners with Pisans and Genoese, who stepped into Venice's shoes in the capital and elsewhere south of the Black Sea. Even the imperial fleets which he constructed increasingly had to be manned by these same Italians as mercenary sailors and captains, since sufficient Greeks were apparently not available for this purpose. In short, Manuel's naval power, though impressive, did not represent any revival of Byzantium's historic maritime strength. Instead, though it was paid for and controlled by this able Comnenian ruler, it was essentially Latin in character and in personnel. Meanwhile, despite the economic revival, most of the profits of the empire's foreign trade also were finding their way into Latin coffers.

In fairness to Manuel, he recognized the danger which use of so many Latins represented for the naval and maritime strength of *Romania*. To deal with this problem he tried to allow such Italians, especially Genoese and Pisans, as had settled in the empire to become what amounted to naturalized Byzantine subjects—a status that many Venetians prior to 1171 had probably already been able to enjoy on a "de facto" basis. Unfortunately, such a policy was terribly unpopular with the generally xenophobic Byzantine population, as became apparent as soon as the strong hand of this greatest of the Comneni emperors was removed from the tiller of the ship of state.

Disaster was not long delayed after Manuel died in 1180. He left as his heir a child under the control of an unpopular western Latin-born empress. Almost at once a cousin, Andronicus Comnenus, emerged as leader of anti-western forces and in 1182 was able to seize control of the capital after a massacre of thousands of Latins who lived there. Andronicus soon disposed of his young cousin and his Latin mother and made himself emperor. His anti-western policies, however, had a disastrous effect upon the fleet, which was largely manned by Italians. Most were either killed in the massacre of the Latins or fled, leaving the fleet paralyzed. By the time a Norman fleet sailed into the Aegean and attacked Salonika in 1185, the powerful armadas of Manuel had been reduced to a few useless, rotting hulls lying at anchor in the Golden Horn.

Andronicus Comnenus was not able to survive the sack of Saloniki, and he was overturned by a coalition of aristocrats, who placed one of their number on the throne as a first Angeli emperor. This new ruler came to terms with the Venetians but was unable to restore Byzantium's fleet. Instead, the Angeli continued powerless upon the sea as the empire started to disintegrate. Distant Trebizond and Cyprus came under the control of members of the Comneni family, and local nobles in Greece and elsewhere made themselves independent of Constantinople. By 1189 when leaders of the Third Crusade began to pass through Byzantine territory on their way to the Holy Land, there was still no fleet available in Constantinople to protect its frontiers, and the Aegean was in the hands of mixed crews of Greeks and Italians, who plundered its sea coasts without interference. Whatever money might have been available for naval purposes was being sent west to the Emperor Henry VI of Germany as a bribe to keep him from attacking Byzantine territory. The Byzantine world lay defenseless without a navy as ominous forces gathered in the west for the Fourth Crusade. Its naval forces, rebuilt so carefully by the Comneni, by 1203 were no longer in existence.

When the Fourth Crusaders sailed to Constantinople in 1203–04, only a few tubs were available in the harbor to defend this great city. As a result, as we shall see later in eye-witness accounts, this great metropolis, which Constantine had made his capital almost nine centuries earlier, fell for the first time into the foreign hands of the Venetians and Latins, who had so long coveted its wealth. Byzantium, once a major naval power in the Mediterranean, had ceased to be important on the sea.

The battle at Constantinople is worthy of comment because it combined naval and military elements. The attacking westerners employed an amphibious operation to storm the walls of the city. Great gangways and bridges were constructed and hoisted up the masts of the attackers' ships, which were anchored at the foot of the sea walls. The connecting walkway permitted the soldiers, or marines, to rush onto the walls and gain access to the city. The use of waterbase attack craft gave the errant Crusaders the advantage by forcing the Byzantines to divide their forces rather than bunch them along the main overland entry to the city.

There remained only a rather sad Byzantine naval postscript lasting almost a century more. After 1204 the Empire found itself partitioned among the Venetians and their Latin allies and emerged divided into western holdings near the sea and three Greek successor states. Only one of these—the Empire of Nicaea—was able to develop any naval strength on a local level along the Asiatic shores of the Aegean between Smyrna and Rhodes. In practice, the waters of *Romania* were now controlled by Venice or by pirate flotillas with mixed Greek and Italian crews, who continued to operate after 1204 much as they had in the decades just before the Fourth Crusade.

Even when the Empire of Nicaea expanded across the Aegean into Thrace and recovered Constantinople in 1261, no Byzantine naval renaissance took place. Instead, the new emperor, Michael Paleologus, attempted to counter the Venetians on the sea with a Genoese alliance and relied upon irregular pirate craft to defend imperial interests—forces that were more dangerous to the empire's inhabitants than to the sea power of its Italian enemies. By 1291, as the last crusading port in Syria fell to the Muslims, the remnant of the Byzantine Empire was without a fleet to defend itself. And so it was to remain until Constantinople finally fell to the Ottoman Turks in 1453. That impressive naval power which Justinian had inaugurated, Heraclians and Isaurians had used so valiantly, and Macedonians and Comneni had relied on so effectively, was no more. With its passing the effective power of the Byzantine Empire ended.

CHAPTER III

Muslim Naval and Maritime Power
in the Mediterranean, 651–1498

IN 651 A NEW ERA began in the Mediterranean when, as noted in our last chapter, Muawiyah, the Ummayad governor of Syria and future caliph, organized a fleet in ports which the Arabs had just captured from the Byzantine Empire in Syria and Egypt and sailed forth to occupy the island of Cyprus. This action began a new phase in Mediterranean maritime and naval history. Although the Arabs had long been acquainted with the sea and had sailed for centuries through the Indian Ocean complex using Indian-type ships and nautical techniques, it seems that from the start in Mediterranean waters they relied on the native Christian population to furnish them with needed ships, crews, and naval expertise. For an account of these activities we have the narrative of al-Baladhuri:

> The first conquest of Cyprus was led on the sea by Mu'áwiyah [Governor of Syria and later Caliph]. Mu'áwiyah had earlier asked Caliph Omar's permission to lead a naval expedition but Omar refused. When Othman became Caliph Mu'áwiyah wrote again asking permission to invade Cyprus informing him of its

proximity and the ease of acquiring it. Othman wrote back "If thou sailest with thy wife we allow thee to do so, otherwise not." Accordingly Mu'áwiyah embarked from there with a large number of ships. This took place in 650 or 651. When the Moslems arrived in Cyprus and landed on its shores, its governor asked to make terms of capitulation. . . . Muáwiyah made terms with them on 7,200 dinars to be paid annually. . . . In the year 32 [654] the Cypriots offered ships as an aid to the Greeks in an expedition at sea. Consequently Mu'áwiyah invaded them in the year 655 with 500 ships. He took Cyprus slaughtering and taking prisoners. He sent to the island 12,000 settlers and built mosques. [Ahmad ibn Jábiral Baladhuri, *The Origins of the Islamic State*, trans. P. Hitti (New York, 1968), I, pp. 235–36.]

Initially, the Arabs had some successes in widely scattered raids culminating in 655 with that great victory off Asia Minor called The Battle of the Masts, which, as we have mentioned already, must have severely crippled the Byzantine naval establishment.

The lull which followed and which allowed the emperors of Constantinople to complete a reorganization of their defenses upon land and sea was not used effectively by the Arabs. Instead the ensuing years saw Muawiyah, the guiding spirit behind this first Muslim naval effort, fully occupied by his struggle with Ali for control of Islam and by the aftermath of that struggle. By the time he was ready to return to the attack, he found that he faced a better organized Byzantine naval establishment capable of dealing with Arab assaults much more effectively.

Between 672 and 678, a first major effort to carry the naval war deep into Byzantine waters ended in a defeat for the Muslim armada as noted in the last chapter. Constantinople was saved, and the Arab, Syrian, and Egyptian flotillas were decimated by Greek fire. There is no evidence, however, that this Muslim defeat ended hostilities for long, and our sources show the Muslims continuing to raid Byzantine shores from Sicily to Cilicia, just as their armies were launching annual *razzias* by land deep into Asia Minor.

The second and supreme Arab naval attack on Constantinople took place in 717–718 after the Arabs, having conquered Carthage and other Tunisian ports from Byzantium, became able to organize a third fleet in the central Mediterranean and as far west as Spain. This second assault, in which all three Arab Mediterranean fleets were involved, was also unsuccessful, as has been noted, because Byzantine diplomacy and naval expertise in the use of Greek fire, combined with the superior leadership of the new Isaurian dynasty, helped to drive the Ummayad fleets out of the Aegean, to which they were not to return for more than a century.

Nevertheless, for some three decades more, a desultory naval war of raid and counter-raid continued between Byzantium and the Arabs until the loss of the latter's eastern Mediterranean fleet in 747 and the bottling up of their Tunisian squadrons ended this hundred-year conflict. By the time the Abbasids had defeated their Ummayad rivals and moved the capital of the Caliphate far from the Mediterranean to Iraq, the waters of the Middle Sea were dominated by Byzantine naval squadrons. We have no record of any considerable flotillas being built subsequently in Syrian and Egyptian ports, which became increasingly moribund from a maritime and commercial point of view, while along Tunisian shores Arab governors built a series of *ribats* or coastal fortresses to protect themselves from attacks from Byzantine Sicily. The Islamic world of the Abbasids turned away from the Mediterranean to a thriving maritime trade with India and China, which provided Baghdad with much of its wealth. If one wished to communicate with North Africa, according to Ibn Khordadbeh's *Book of Routes*, one now traveled from Egypt to the Maghreb (northwest Africa) by camel caravan instead of by sea.

What was the nature of this first unsuccessful Muslim naval effort in the Mediterranean, and what kind of ships did it entail? We do not know for sure. It does seem, however, that in composition and tactics Muslim flotillas were quite similar to those of their Byzantine opponents and were unlike those used by Arab merchants in the Indian Ocean. Since much of their activity consisted of raiding, Muslim Mediterranean flotillas of warships included more fast, oared vessels and fewer sailing *naves* than was the case for their Byzantine naval rivals, but the overall organization of Muslim fleets very much resembled that of Byzantine fleets. For instance, the Tunisian flotilla, down to the middle of the eighth century, was very much the counterpart of Constantinople's Sicilian squadron; the Syrian Arab fleet matched Byzantine's themal naval forces at the mouth of the Aegean and along the south coast of Asia Minor (the theme of the Karrabisians); and the Egyptian fleet built in dockyards at Alexandria and up the Nile near the island of Roda was quite similar to the imperial fleet which was maintained in the Golden Horn.

There were, however, also several differences between these two naval establishments. During this Ummayad period, there is no evidence that Arab ships ever used Greek fire, which remained Constantinople's secret weapon. In addition, the Arabs suffered from a severe deficiency in wood necessary for naval construction, especially in the eastern Mediterranean. Indeed, it may well have been this lack of ship timber upon which Byzantium finally capitalized about 700, when she instituted a system of trade controls. Byzantium had discovered the Achilles heel of this first Arab effort on the sea. The relationship between forests and sea power was no less crucial to modern western states as late as the nineteenth century.

For the last three-quarters of the eighth century, things were quiet on the sea. Byzantine squadrons kept the Arabs penned up in their coastal towns and discouraged their foreign trade, except under strict controls. Partly as a result of this Byzantine blockade, the caliphs of Baghdad were unable to maintain political control of their western provinces. First Spain, then Morocco, and then Tunis became increasingly autonomous under local dynasties of emirs, and even Egypt proved extremely difficult to control. The Arab Mediterranean world was a depressed area very different from the thriving condition of its more eastern Red Sea and Persian Gulf regions.

In the first decades of the ninth century, this situation changed suddenly and dramatically. The change began when, during a revival of religious arguments over the use of icons, serious revolts disturbed the reign of the Emperor Michael II in Constantinople. In the west the entire Sicilian fleet, commanded by the Admiral Euphemius, deserted to the North African Aghlabid emirs of Tunisia, while in the east disorders and civil war resulted in the all but complete destruction of those themal fleets which had so long guarded the entrance to the Aegean.

As a result of these internal Byzantine disorders, the Aghlabids in 827 began a slow but steady conquest of the island of Sicily, beginning with Palermo and culminating with the fall of Syracuse in 878. Even more important was the seizure of Crete in 826 by a small body of Spanish Muslim pirates, who for a decade had controlled the city of Alexandria. Soon thereafter Cyprus again became Muslim, and Corsica, Sardinia, and the Balearics in the west came under Islamic control. As the islands of the Mediterranean became Islamic, a series of more advanced pirate bases was established along the northern shores of the Middle Sea at Fraxinetum in Provence, Monte Garigliano near Naples, in and around Bari in Apulia, and even in Attica in the Aegean. Byzantine naval power suddenly found itself penned up in the northern Adriatic, the northern Aegean, and the Black Sea, while Muslim merchant vessels could sail undisturbed to Spain and Morocco from Egypt and Syria by way of Sicily and the Tunisian coast.

How did the Islamic world proceed to organize its naval power in the Mediterranean, which it so largely dominated through the tenth century? In analyzing this dominance, we must begin by distinguishing rather sharply between an outer screen of pirate raiders located at Tortosa, the Balearics, and Fraxinetum in the west; Sicily, Monte Garigliano, and Bari in the center; and Crete, Cyprus, and Cilicia in the east, and Islam's more organized regular naval establishments. Its pirate fleets were essentially *ghazi* raiding forces operating on the sea in regular *razzias* against Latin and Greek Christian territory, much as similar *ghazis* did along Spanish or Armenian land frontiers. Sometimes, of course, these raids took the form of a major naval expedition, such as that which captured Salonika in 904. More often they operated on a smaller scale. But whatever their character, they served to keep their Christian opponents penned up while leaving the major portion of the Mediterranean safe for peaceful Muslim trading vessels traveling along southern maritime routes between east and west.

Behind this pirate screen, however, lay the main Muslim fleets, which, by the early tenth century, consisted of two important armadas: one controlled by the Ummayads of Spain and Morocco and the other, the Fatimid fleet of Algeria and Tunis. A third and less-important fleet was that of the Ikhshids of Egypt and Syria. These naval forces consisted of a large number of warships built in special dockyards, manned by professional sailors, and commanded by regular admirals—much like the imperial fleet of the nearby Byzantine Empire. Such flotillas were mainly not concerned with raids upon Christian shores. Instead, they watched each other as rivals, though that of the Ummayads had as a secondary mission the protection of Atlantic shores from European Viking attacks.

Particularly aggressive was the fleet of the Fatimids, who had designs on both the domains of the Ummayads in the west and those of the Ikhshids in the east. Finally in 969, after two great attacks failed, the Fatimids were able to conquer the Valley of the Nile using their

fleet and to extend their authority north into Syria and south into the
Red Sea from their new capital of Cairo, thus emerging as the leading
Islamic naval power in the Mediterranean.

The intense rivalry between these Muslim states had two byprod-
ucts worth noting. The major Muslim fleets were so busy watching
each other that they never organized any control of trade passing
along their Mediterranean shores similar to that which had long been
practiced by the Byzantine Empire in waters it controlled. Muslim
merchant shipping could sail from east to west through the Middle
Sea relatively undisturbed, as information from Geniza traders in
Cairo makes quite clear. This rivalry also explains why the Byzantine
fleet in the 960s was able to retake Crete, Cilicia, and Cyprus, for the
Fatimids and Ikhshids were so busy with their own rivalry that they
could give no naval assistance to their co-religionists attempting to
hold such advanced pirate bases.

What emerged then from a maritime and commercial point of
view for the Islamic world of the Mediterranean now needs to be examined. By the early tenth century, Muslim merchants began to sail
through the Mediterranean in great seasonal convoys, which linked
every Islamic shore with every other. These great maritime routes
were linked with a number of caravan routes that crossed the Sahara
from the south and brought gold from the Sudan to Maghrebi shores,
further stimulating commerce. Timber, which was in short supply
earlier, was now available in a number of western Spanish or North
African locations and could be easily shipped to the wood-deficient
eastern Mediterranean area of Egypt and Syria. Trade from the Red
Sea to the Indian Ocean became increasingly important and began to
integrate the Islamic Mediterranean economic area with that of the
Indian Ocean. An age of affluence began throughout the Muslim
Mediterranean as new Oriental agricultural crops, such as cotton,
sugar, and citrus fruits, were introduced, new industrial and mining
ventures mushroomed, and new towns and cities grew in importance.
The whole Islamic world from Central Asia and Malaya to the Atlantic became the greatest free-trade area the world had ever known. Its
gold *dinar* currency, accepted everywhere, became the dollar of the
period. The days of Byzantine naval control of Mediterranean commerce became a thing of the past in the Islamic parts of the Mediterranean.

But even this peaceful Mediterranean contained perils as the
following letter of an eleventh-century Jewish trader makes clear.

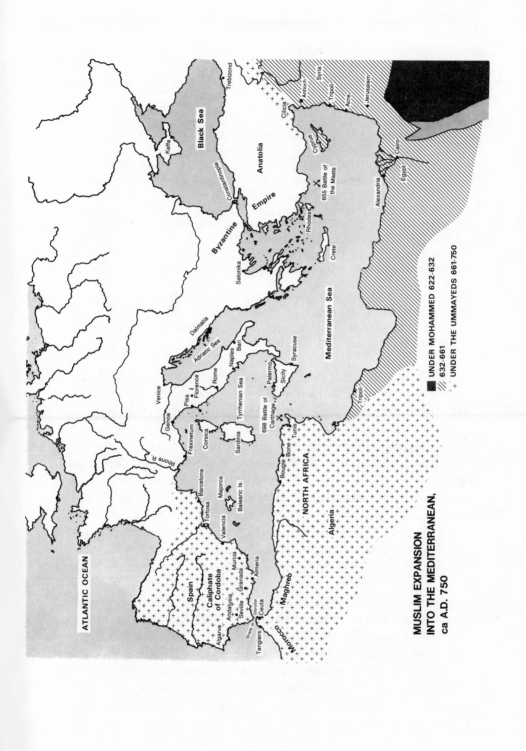

MUSLIM EXPANSION
INTO THE MEDITERRANEAN,
ca A.D. 750

■ UNDER MOHAMMED 622-632
▨ 632-661
▨ UNDER THE UMMAYEDS 661-750

ATLANTIC OCEAN

Spain
Caliphate
of Cordoba
Algarve
Andalusia
Seville
Granada
Almeria
Murcia
Valencia
Tortosa
Barcelona
Majorca
Balearic Is.
Gibraltar
Strait of
Ceuta
Tangiers
MOROCCO
Maghreb
NORTH AFRICA
Algeria
Tunis
Bone
Bougie

Rhone R.
Genoa
Venice
Pisa
Florence
Rome
Naples
Fraxinetum
Corsica
Sardinia
Tyrrhenian Sea
Bari
Palermo
Sicily
Syracuse
698 Battle of
Carthage
Tripoli

Dalmatia
Adriatic Sea
Salonika

Mediterranean Sea

Crete
Rhodes

Byzantine
Empire
Anatolia

Kaffa
Black Sea
Constantinople
Trebizond

Cyprus
655 Battle of
the Masts

Antioch
Syria
Tripoli
Acre
Jerusalem

Cilicia
Alexandria
Cairo
Egypt

I faced death and unbearable dangers from the day I parted
from my parents. . . . We arrived in Palermo on the [. . .] and paid
customs on everything in addition to duties imposed on us for
the . . . of the sailors of the ship. We were [there] a week and
waited. Finally we found a large ship there which sailed to Alexandria, Egypt. We paid the fare and embarked before the New
Year holiday. But on the fifth of the month of Tishri [September]
on Monday at noon time, a storm broke loose upon us [. . .],
storming upon us for three days. On the third day the ship began
to leak and water penetrated into it from all sides. [We worked
hard] to reduce its load and to bail the water out, for there was a
big crowd on the ship, about 400 persons [. . .]. The sea became
ever wilder and the ship was tossed about with its entire load. All
the people lay down . . . [and cried to] God. Then they approached
the captain and pleaded with him saying "Save us! Turn the ship
toward the land . . . before the sun sets when everything will be
lost. . . ." The ship was steered towards the coast. . . . Finally the
ship touched ground and cracked asunder, as [an egg] would
crack when a man presses it with his two hands. [*Letters of
Medieval Jewish Traders*, trans. S.D. Goitein (Princeton, 1973),
pp. 40–41.]

One thing, however, is still in doubt: the kinds of ships used during
this period in Muslim navies or by Muslim merchants. We know,
thanks to the existence of Geniza records, that the vessels on which
merchants sailed with their goods were varied in size, shape, and sailing characteristics—some of them being very large and others
smaller, such as the sunken eleventh-century Islamic ship, loaded
with a cargo of glass, found off the coast of Asia Minor at Serçe Liman
and now being examined by underwater archeologists. We have less
information concerning warships, except that they must have resembled Byzantine oared *dromons* of the period or the various transports
used by Nicephorus Phocas in his invasion of Crete. We also know
that once they were established in Egypt after 970, the Fatimids built larger
warships similar to those constructed earlier by Romanus
Lecapenus for his fleet in Constantinople. With a fleet composed of
these larger warships and armed with Greek fire and catapults and
other war machines, the Fatimid navy from 975 on was able to fight
its Byzantine opponents on equal terms in waters off Sicily and Syria.

This age of Islamic naval strength and economic maritime affluence, however, did not extend much beyond the first decades of the
eleventh century. It ended in part because of a failure of Islamic gov-

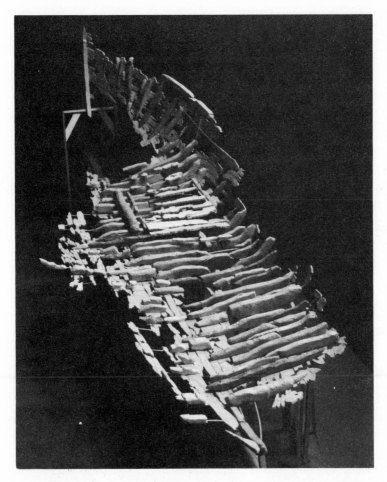

Reconstruction of an eleventh-century vessel, loaded with glass, found at Serçe Liman off the southwest coast of Turkey. This ship is an important example of the conversion to frame-first construction rather than completing the hull and then inserting ribs. Fragment model by J. Richard Steffy, Institute of Nautical Archaeology, Texas A & M University.

ernments. During the ninth and tenth centuries Muslim rulers everywhere had come to rely upon slave and mercenary troops to keep order in their cities, serve in their armies, and man their organized fleets. In the eleventh century, these troops began to turn on their masters and tear apart the states they were supposed to protect from internal disorder or foreign foes. In turn, nomadic tribesmen from

Section of the hull of the Serçe Liman ship. She was rated at 37
tons burden with a length of 15 m. and beam of 5.13 m. Probably
an Arab merchantman, she carried Byzantine amphorae and Arab
utensils for the crew. Drawing by J. Richard Steffy.

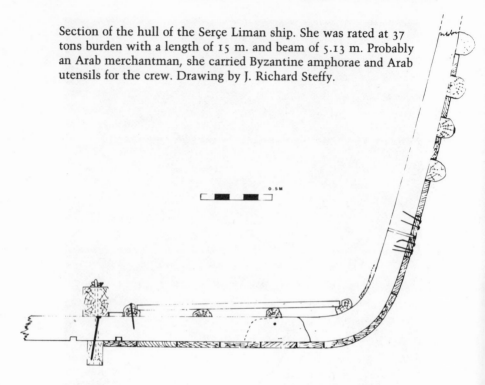

desert areas began to invade settled regions no longer able to defend
themselves.

This breakdown of order happened first in the west, where by 1025
the Caliphate of Cordova had disappeared and its place been taken by
a series of regional principalities called *taifas*, and in Morocco, which
fell into the hands of nomadic invaders from the Sahara desert.

A few years later it was the turn of the Fatimid Empire, from
which Sicily, Algeria, and Tunis became independent about 1050.
Cairo was convulsed by slave revolts, and the nomadic Arab tribes
which had invaded Syria and Egypt went on to attack Tunisia in force.
At the same time, eastern Islamic areas also found themselves unable
to maintain stable governments and so opened their gates to Seljuk
Turkish tribesmen, who, by 1055, controlled Persia and Iraq and in
the 1070s began to advance deep into Byzantine Asia Minor and
northern Syria as well.

This chaos and political instability resulted in the disintegration
of the Muslim flotillas which had for so many decades controlled the

waters of the Middle Sea from organized bases and left advanced pirate bases exposed to hostile attack as well. Indeed, by the time the First Crusade was launched in 1096, the only relatively effective Mediterranean naval establishment still in existence was that of Fatimid Egypt, and this was a pale shadow of what it had been some eight or nine decades earlier. Muslim naval weakness and governmental failure in the Middle Sea were now as marked as those of its Byzantine neighbors.

In the light of this, it is not surprising that Latin Europe during the eleventh century began to expand in the Mediterranean at the expense of the Islamic world. This Latin expansion was carried out by various combinations of feudal noble adventurers and new Italian sea power, which often had the backing of a revived and aggressive western papacy. In Muslim Iberia, now reduced to a number of weak and quarrelling principalities, the Latin advance took the form of an expansion south of the Duero River. The Christian states extorted large sums of money in the form of tribute payments, and Islamic Spain became so weak on the sea that it could no longer keep northern European ships from sailing through the Strait of Gibraltar with complete impunity.

In the central Mediterranean, we find Pisa and Genoa suddenly developing some piratical naval muscle which by 1050 was able to clear Corsica and Sardinia of Muslims, help the Normans begin to take over Sicily, and in 1087 launch a great plundering expedition, which sacked the port of Medhia along the coast of Tunisia. The eleventh century also saw the emergence of Norman states in Sicily and southern Italy with considerable naval strength—the work of the talented Guiscard family. And last of all, this period saw the emergence of Venice, which was powerful enough on the sea to dominate the Illyrian coast of the Adriatic and to help Byzantium expel aggressive Normans from Albanian shores in the 1080s.

When a Byzantine plea for help against the Seljuk Turks resulted in the First Crusade, the successful planting of a series of Latin crusading states in Syria and Palestine allowed the Genoese, Pisans, and Venetians to establish themselves firmly in seaport cities which belonged to the Kingdom of Jerusalem. By 1100 the waters of the Middle Sea had largely passed into the hands of Latin Christians along with a number of the more important islands, such as Corsica, Sardinia, Malta, and Sicily, and Italian traders could travel relatively freely along seaways previously dominated by Islamic navies and merchant shipping. With this change, that great wave of prosperity which had characterized the Islamic world of the Mediterranean since the late ninth and tenth centuries came to a temporary end.

During the first part of the twelfth century, Latin westerners continued their expansion at the expense of Islam in a number of areas of the Middle Sea. After a lull, during which the Almoravids of Morocco crossed the Straits of Gibraltar, halted the Christian advance into southern Spain, and regained control of the Atlantic and Mediterranean waters east and west of Ceuta, the Christian *Reconquista* resumed. Lisbon was taken by crusading fleets from England and the Low Countries; Tortosa and Almeria were captured by the Genoese with the help of Spanish and Provinçal noble contingents, and the Balearic Islands were temporarily occupied by a Pisan expedition.

Around mid-century, Roger II of Sicily was able to seize almost every important Muslim port in North Africa between Tripoli and Bougie using a large, well-organized fleet. At the same time, the Pisans, Genoese, and Venetians helped the kings of Jerusalem capture every Muslim port along the coast of Syria north of Ascalon, while in 1128 the navy of Venice annihilated the fleet of Fatimid Egypt off the coast of Palestine. By 1140 Muslim sea power in the Mediterranean seemed at an end.

Then a Muslim rally on land and sea began, which was to last through the rest of the century. It started in the west, where in 1147 the Almoravids were replaced in Morocco by the more effective, fanatical Almohad movement. These Almohads were able by the 1160s to extend their rule over the entire Maghreb and to build a fleet strong enough to expel the Normans from ports in Tripoli, Tunisia, and Algeria. Victorious in North Africa, they moved across the straits, where they united the Muslims in Spain and halted the Christian advance to the south. By the end of the century they controlled a great empire on both sides of the straits and had a fleet which dominated the waters of the Atlantic south of Cape Vincent and of the western Mediterranean south of the Balearics.

In the eastern Mediterranean, a new Muslim leader named Saladin appeared about 1170, who was able to replace the Fatimids in Cairo and in the Red Sea area, while uniting Muslim Syria and Egypt. Once firmly in control, he rebuilt the Egyptian fleet and in 1187 advanced into Palestine, where he destroyed the army of the Kingdom of

Jerusalem at the battle of Hattin. Two years later the Holy City of Jerusalem was his, and most of the ports along the coast had been captured by his fleet and army.

Saladin's success, however, resulted in the Third Crusade, which limited his gains considerably. The English fleet of Richard I helped to destroy the naval power he had built up in Egypt as is seen in the following account:

> On the sixteenth of Jomada I (i.e., 11 June 1191) there came to Beyrout (Beirut) a ship of vast size, laden with warlike implements, with arms, provisions, and valiant men. . . . It held six hundred and fifty valiant men of war; but the English (king) sunk it after surrounding it with a fleet of forty sail. . . . The Captain . . . saw that all things boded imminent disaster and that there was no way of escaping death, he called aloud: "By Allah, we will seek a noble death; and we will not yield even the smallest morsel of our craft into the hands of the foe." Thus he spoke; and those on board began straightway with axes to cleave and bore through their own vessel; until they had, as it were, flung wide the gates by which the water might enter on every side. All men on board were drowned and with them went down the warlike gear, the victuals, and everything else, so the enemy carried off no booty. Now the name of this Captain was Jacob of Aleppo. [From Beda ad-Din, *Life of Saladin*, 102 in T.A. Archer, *The Crusade of Richard I* (London, 1888), pp. 77–78.]

The Latin westerners were able to recover all the coastal cities they had lost. But Jerusalem and the interior of Syria and Palestine remained in Muslim hands and united with Egypt under the control of Saladin's successors. Thus united, they formed a strong barrier to further Latin Christian advances. In the eastern Mediterranean, as in its western waters, the last part of the twelfth century was a period of Muslim success.

How did this century of Christian advance and the subsequent Muslim reaction to it affect Islamic maritime civilization in the Mediterranean? These years saw a considerable revival of the kind of prosperity which the disordered eleventh century had curtailed. The Christian Spanish realms, the Norman Kingdom of Sicily, and the crusading states of Syria, as well as the ubiquitous merchants of Pisa, Genoa, and Venice, were initially more interested in joining in the prosperity of the Muslim world than they were in destroying it. The *dinar* continued to hold sway in the eastern Mediterranean and in

A modern *boom* made in Kuwait, photographed in the 1950s. It is
remarkably similar to the vessels constructed by the Arabs centuries ago. In 1979–80 an 87′ handcrafted replica of a ship that might
have been sailed by Sindbad, the legendary sailor of *The Arabian
Nights*, was constructed in Oman under the direction of naval ar-
chitect Colin Mudie and Tim Severin, who sailed it 6000 miles to
Guangzhou (Canton). No nails were used, and the ship was held together by cordage made from the fibers of coconut husks. Photo by
Wilfred Thesiger, from *Arabian Sands*, by permission of Viking
Penguin, Inc.

Sicily as did the Almohad *maraboutin* in western waters. Muslim
merchants such as Ibn Jaybaur traveled freely on Latin ships, and
Latin courts in Palermo and Toledo prized Islamic culture. Muslim
mercenaries could serve in the armies and navies of Norman Sicily or
of the Kingdom of Jerusalem, while Spanish Christian militia could
prop up the regimes of the Almoravids and Almohads in Morocco.
Islamic merchant ships still plied the Mediterranean in convoys,
though increasingly they felt the competition of their Italian rivals.
Down to 1200 the basic patterns of trade which developed in that
tenth–century age of affluence had returned to the Muslim Mediterranean after an eleventh-century hiatus.

   Then came the thirteenth century, which was to prove especially
disastrous for the Islamic Mediterranean world east and west. In 1212

in the Iberian Peninsula a joint effort by most of the Christian monarchs resulted in a disastrous Muslim defeat at the battle of Las Navas de Tolosa. This Christian victory was not followed up at once, but in 1229 King Jaume of Aragon began a conquest of Majorca, which was completed six years later, and in 1236 King Ferdinand III of Castile moved south and captured Cordova. Both rulers continued their advances, Jaume proceeding with the conquest of Valencia, while Castile absorbed Murcia and all Andalusia except the mountain kingdom of Granada, which remained Moorish. Especially important was the capture of the great port of Seville, which fell into the hands of Ferdinand in 1248. Meanwhile, the Portuguese were also advancing south to absorb the Algarve. By 1250, although the Moors still held territory on both sides of the Straits of Gibraltar, effective power on both sides of the passage between the Atlantic and Mediterranean had passed into Latin hands.

The next half century saw the Christian Spanish realms continue to exploit their victories. Aragonese and Genoese who had helped the Castilians take Seville continued to patrol the straits and to advance out into the Atlantic west of Morocco, while in the Mediterranean, the Catalans replaced the Pisans and their rivals, the Genoese, as the dominant naval power along the shores of North Africa from Tripoli to Ceuta. The Catalans even began to play a special role of providing the Muslim rulers of Tunis and Algeria with Christian bodyguards, who were the mainstay of their rule. Though a few Muslim and Jewish merchants continued to operate in western Mediterranean waters, the great Islamic fleets of earlier centuries were no longer in existence. Only a few pirate craft, often manned by Muslims expelled from Spain and bitter about their expulsion, continued to maintain Islamic naval traditions. Control of the sea and the commercial exploitation of all maritime trading activities was now in Latin Christian hands.

In the eastern Mediterranean, except for a few Turkish pirates operating along Anatolian shores, a similar picture of western Latin naval dominance was emerging. The Third and Fourth Crusades had seen the demise of Byzantine sea power in the east, and there was a similar decline of Islamic fleets. Saladin's heirs never were able to rebuild the fleet lost in 1190, which explains why Latin Crusaders were able to seize the Egyptian port of Damietta in both the Fifth and Sixth Crusades without encountering any hostile naval contingents. It also helps us to understand why, when the Fifth Crusade met disaster in Egypt, the Kingdom of Jerusalem could still extend its borders until it was almost as large as it had been before Saladin attacked it a few decades earlier. The Sultan of Egypt faced up to the strategic consequences of poor naval support and surrendered the city of Jerusalem in 1229 without a fight, in the face of the overwhelming naval power which Emperor Frederick II of Sicily was able to muster along Egyptian shores.

Even after 1250, when the Ayyubids of Egypt had been replaced by Mamluk Sultans, no real Muslim sea power was at first reestablished in these waters. Instead, the slow, steady reconquest of the coastal, crusader-controlled cities of Palestine and Syria by the Mamluks took place without using sea power at all. When Acre fell in 1291, it was because of military, not naval, force. Indeed, so little confidence did these Mamluks have in their ability to deal with the sea that they dismantled the fortification of almost every Syrian port that they re-captured. By 1300 in their domains there had been a dramatic retreat from the sea. Islamic economic power now centered in interior cities such as Cairo, Aleppo, and Damascus, rather than along Mediterra-nean shores, where only Alexandria and Beirut still were maintained as portals facing a hostile Latin-controlled Middle Sea.

When the entire Mediterranean–Black Sea area became by 1250, a Latin lake, those great seasonal convoys which for almost four centuries had linked Egypt and Syria with North Africa, Sicily, and Spain ceased to exist. Geniza records in Egypt of this commerce ceased about midcentury. In place of the gold *dinar* and the gold *nomisma*, which had been the great international mediums of ex-change for the Islamic and Byzantine worlds, respectively, we now find Italian gold florins and ducats, representing the economic domi-nance of Florence and Venice, beginning to be universally employed. A new maritime and commercial world had appeared in Mediterra-nean waters along with dominant western naval forces.

Why did the older Islamic civilization fail to survive in a naval and maritime sense during this century—a failure almost as decisive, it seems, as that of nearby Byzantium. We can ascribe this state of affairs to three basic failures. The first was governmental. While western European governments on all levels were developing bureaucracies and institutions which used advanced financial plan-ning, government in the Islamic world increasingly relied upon slave contingents such as the Egyptian Mamluks or upon tribal elements. Western Latin states, as a result, had the funds and know-how to build and maintain expensive naval fleets. The Islamic world did not.

Second, the Islamic world failed to match the economic and commercial advances which characterized thirteenth-century Europe—especially Italy, Catalonia, and southern France. Its merchants never progressed beyond the simple *commenda*-like partnership and were strangers to double-entry bookkeeping, extensive use of credit instruments, banking, and marine insurance. They could not, therefore, compete commercially on the sea with their Latin rivals any more than they could in a naval sense. The only advantage they had was the use of Arabic numerals for business purposes, a practice which the Italians adopted before the century had ended.

Finally, the Islamic world, like that of Byzantium, fell hopelessly behind the Latin west in its maritime technology. Muslims in the Mediterranean developed no new ship types like the *cogs* which entered these waters from the north, or like those which were developed in Iberian waters to become the Atlantic *caravel* of the future. They seem to have lagged in their use of the stern rudder—except in the Indian Ocean. And there is no evidence that they adopted the portolan chart or the boxed compass, which revolutionized Latin Europe's Mediterranean shipping practices. As a result, they could compete with their Latin rivals only in the building of swift corsair craft, which could be used only in special maritime situations along the trade routes. From Tana and Trebizond on the Black Sea and Famagusta on Cyprus to Gibraltar and beyond, these waters had become a preserve of western Europe by 1300 if not by 1250.

The Islamic world's backwardness in the naval and maritime sphere continued into the fourteenth century—especially since the Latin west continued to increase its governmental, economic, and technological lead. For instance, the relatively inexpensive crossbows and catapults of earlier times began to be replaced by cannons and gunpowder in sea battles. Ships became larger and larger, whether employed in warfare or in trade. Lacking the dockyards and technical skills of a Venice or of a Barcelona, the Islamic world could not compete with such craft or arm its own ships to meet westerners in battle with any hope of success, as was seen in 1365, when Alexandria fell to a crusading force without any serious effort to defend itself.

Nevertheless, in certain areas of the Mediterranean, the Islamic world scored a few successes, which showed it still maintained some maritime vitality of its own. For example, in 1339–1340 the Merinids of Morocco briefly reunited all of the Maghreb, expelled the Christian militias, who had long maintained local sultans in power, and crossed into southern Spain with a sizeable force.

Their attack on Andalusia was unsuccessful. A joint Castilian-Portuguese force defeated their army at the battle of Salado in 1340, while Latin naval forces regained naval control of the Strait of Gibraltar. A year or so later their control of Algeria and Tunisia was ended, and they retreated back into Morocco. But their efforts had not been completely in vain, for Latin Christian control of North African shores had been profoundly shaken and piracy increased everywhere. The Barbary Coast became a lair of pirates and increasingly menacing to the Latin west into the next century.

A somewhat similar situation developed along Syrian and Egyptian shores. This region remained relatively unimportant, commercially speaking, during the first decades of the fourteenth century because Latin merchants tended to receive silks, spices, and other eastern wares via the Persian Gulf, instead of by way of the Red Sea. Goods from the Persian Gulf passed to ports in Lesser Armenia, just north of Latin-held Cyprus, or to Trebizond in the Black Sea. In some cases commerce with China proceeded over land to Kaffa or Tana along the northern shores of the Euxine. These routes were favored because the Mongol Empire had, since about 1250, linked these areas together commercially.

In 1346 Mongol rule ended in Persia, and by 1368, it had ended in China as well. Routes reaching the Black Sea or Mediterranean via the Persian Gulf or central Asia became increasingly difficult, and those traversing the Red Sea were used more frequently. Egypt, in general, and Alexandria, in particular, again became *the* entrepôt for the Mediterranean spice trade, while Beirut became revitalized providing the Latin west with the cottons it needed.

The southward shift of trade routes from the Far East revived Mamluk Egypt's interest in sea power—an interest also stimulated by the brutal Latin sacking of Alexandria in 1365. In retaliation, a small but effective fleet was created and used to exact tribute from Cyprus in 1368 and to attack Lesser Armenia. By the last years of the century, a Mamluk fleet existed in the Mediterranean, which, though it was incapable of challenging the naval forces of the Italians, had some importance of its own.

During the later fourteenth century, the Turkish *ghazi* emirs, who operated along the shores of Anatolia, became much bolder and more dangerous in their raids against commercial shipping and Aegean shores in general. The raids continued even after the crusading order of *Knights Hospitalers* moved its headquarters to Rhodes with the specific objective of curbing Turkish piratical attacks. The rivalry between the Genoese and Venetians in these waters made any real cooperation to suppress such piracy impossible, and so permitted the Turks to develop those maritime skills that were to contribute to the success of the later Ottoman navy.

During the first half of the fifteenth century the tempo of Barbary piracy increased in the west, despite the Portuguese seizure of Ceuta in 1415, while in the eastern Mediterranean the Mamluks continued to maintain a small but efficient navy.

A new element was introduced, however, by the spread of the Ottoman Turks into the Balkans and Asia Minor from their original nucleus in northwestern Anatolia—an expansion which was partly the result of their having a superior army and partly because most of the Greeks and Slavs who submitted to them found their rule preferable to that of the Latin west with its concomitant economic exploitation and religious intolerance.

The fall of Constantinople to the Ottomans in 1453 is explained to us in the following firsthand account.

> Since he (the Ottoman Sultan) was unable to penetrate the harbor (the Golden Horn) by sea and attack the city in this way from all sides, he hit upon the plan of dragging his ships past the camp of Zagan Pasha and running them down into the harbor. In this way he dragged part of his fleet over the hill with sails hoisted and oars moving until they set down to the harbor beach. He transported some seventy vessels in this manner of thirty or forty oars, all ready to set sail in the harbor.
> ... When the Greeks saw the ships all in readiness along the shore of the harbor they decided to man the vessels which were available and attack them to burn them if possible. But the Turks saw them coming and fired their cannon hitting two of their thirty oared vessels which sunk immediately drowning those of their crews who could not swim. The Turkish ships which had been dragged across to the harbor now took to the water and no one could prevent them from attacking the city. [Laonicus Chalcocondylos, *Turkish History* VIII, trans. J. Melville in *The Siege of Constantinople*, 1453. *Seven Contemporary Chronicles* (Amsterdam, 1972), pp. 45–46.]

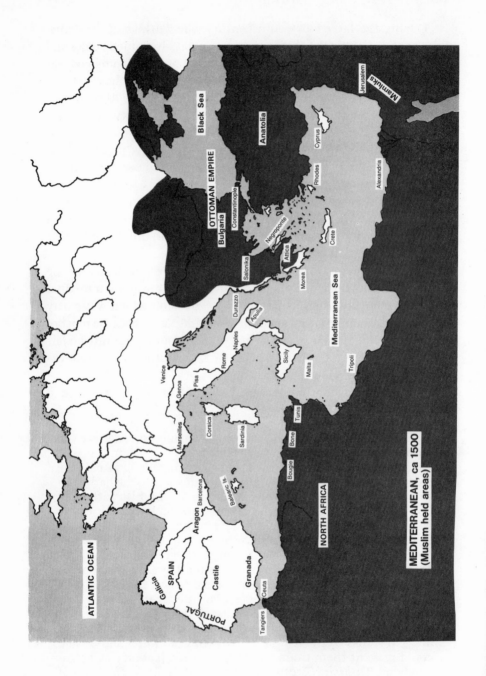

ATLANTIC OCEAN

PORTUGAL

SPAIN
Galicia
Castile
Aragon
Barcelona
Granada
Ceuta
Tangiers

Balearic Is.
Marseilles
Corsica
Sardinia

Venice
Genoa
Pisa
Rome
Naples
Apulia
Durazzo

Sicily
Malta
Bougie
Bone
Tunis
Tripoli

NORTH AFRICA

Mediterranean Sea

Salonika
Morea
Attica
Negroponte
Crete
Rhodes
Cyprus
Alexandria

OTTOMAN EMPIRE
Bulgaria
Constantinople
Anatolia

Black Sea

Jerusalem
Mamluks

MEDITERRANEAN, ca 1500
(Muslim held areas)

The capture of Constantinople by the Turks changed things dramatically. The Byzantine Empire came to an end, the Black Sea became an Ottoman lake, and a new fleet began to be constructed in dockyards near Constantinople. In a sense, what occurred was a restoration of Byzantine sea power, quiescent since 1291, but now under Ottoman direction. By the 1490s, when Ferdinand and Isabella united Castile and Aragon and led their armies to a conquest of Granada, a new fleet rode at anchor in the Golden Horn at Istanbul (formerly Constantinople). The fleet was formidable and a serious threat to Latin, particularly Venetian, shipping. The Adriatic Sea was breached by the Turks, who raided along the Italian coast up to the very perimeters of Venice. A new era was dawning in the Mediterranean which was to threaten the naval preponderance that the Italians and other Latin westerners had enjoyed for two centuries.

Until the last years of the fifteenth century, however, the Islamic retreat from the sea in the face of Western Europe's economic, governmental, and technological maritime superiority was the most important event that had taken place in these waters. And it was this preponderance which was transferred into the Atlantic to become the basis of Europe's imperial destiny in the seven seas of the wider world.

Latin Western Naval Power and Shipping in the Mediterranean, 800–1498

THE LATIN WEST, which was to play such an important role in the Mediterranean by the time of the First Crusade, was very slow to emerge as a naval and maritime center of any importance. Indeed, we find no evidence of any maritime initiative there until the last years of the reign of Charlemagne. Then two areas under Carolingian control in the western Mediterranean began to show some precocious naval muscle. One of them lay along the Catalan coast, which had been newly conquered from the Muslims and where a fleet commanded by a Count of Ampurias was strong enough to defeat Muslim border flotillas and gain control of the Balearics. Though only once again, in 898, were such flotillas reported active along the eastern shores of Iberia, this naval power was certainly the forerunner of later Catalan and Provençal shipping.

Similarly, we find that Carolingian Pisa was able to muster sufficient strength on the sea for its counts to seize the island of Corsica briefly about 816 and ten years later, in 826, raid Bone on the shores of North Africa. Whatever occasioned these brief flurries of

Latin activity on the sea was soon neutralized by the Muslim occupation of the Balearics, by raids in the Tyrrhenian Sea by Islamic freebooters from Sicily and by advanced Muslim bases at Fraxinetum and Maguio on both sides of the Rhone River delta. True maritime strength in this part of the western, Latin Mediterranean had to await the eleventh century.

Much more crucial, at least initially, was the development of two other areas, nominally Byzantine, which by the ninth century possessed some autonomous naval and maritime importance: Venice in the Adriatic and the Naples-Amalfi area in the Tyrrhenian Sea. Of the two, Venice was certainly the more important. She owed her existence to the end of Ravenna as a Byzantine–controlled entrepôt and to the withdrawal of some of the inhabitants of this region to a series of lagoons and low-lying islands just north of the mouth of the Po River. By 800 her inhabitants, ruled by their own Doge, had formed a center of some commercial importance, acquired by trading salt along the shores of the Adriatic and up the Po and by procuring spices and other oriental wares in Constantinople or distant Alexandria. To pay for such wares, they began as early as the first years of the ninth century to ship timber, weapons, and slaves to Islamic ports and thus developed a considerable fleet of their own. During these years the Venetians generally cooperated with Byzantium in suppressing pirates who interfered with their trading along Dalmatian shores, and they played a major role in ending the Muslim occupation of Bari in the 870s. They were less enthusiastic, however, in accepting Byzantine trade controls that limited commerce, essential to their prosperity, with Carolingian Italy or Muslim Egypt. Like the American colonists on the eve of the American Revolution in relation to Britain's navigation acts, the Venetians tended to obey Constantinople's regulations against shipping arms and timber to Muslim ports when it suited their interests or when they needed Byzantine assistance against threats from the mainland. Otherwise, they ignored them.

What was true of Venice was even more true of Naples and Amalfi, which flourished as ports that supplied Byzantine and Muslim oriental wares to Rome and nearby areas in the Tyrrhenian Sea, and shipped timber, slaves, and other wares to Muslim ports in return. But, whereas a large portion of Venetian trade was with the Byzantine Empire, only a fraction of that of the Naples-Amalfi area was so directed. Therefore, except when Byzantine armies and naval contingents were actually present, Naples and Amalfi tended to be much more part of the Arab world, economically speaking, than of the Byzantine Empire. Regardless of the political situation, none of these cities ever stopped trading with Byzantium's Arab enemies. By 1025, for instance, Amalfi had colonies of its merchants located in the Maghreb, Sicily, Egypt, and Syria; and Venice, which now controlled Dalmatia, was almost equally committed to commerce with the prosperous economic realm of Mediterranean Islam.

During the last three quarters of the eleventh century, significant changes occurred. Pisa and Genoa revived as centers of maritime activity. They drove the Muslims from Corsica and Sardinia, helped the Normans take Palermo and other ports in Sicily, and raided North African shores. By 1087 they were joined by Amalfitans in a great naval expedition which sacked the Tunisian city of Medhia. Their pirate fleets became the terror of the western Mediterranean.

All this activity coincided with the arrival of large numbers of Norman adventurers in southern Italy, where, led by Robert and Roger Guiscard, they took control of the entire region south of Rome away from its Byzantine and Lombard rulers. By midcentury the Guiscards had managed to get their power regularized through recognition by both Pope and German Emperor, and, in 1071, they were able to take Bari, the last Byzantine holding in Apulia. Robert Guiscard, the older of the two brothers, then organized the naval strength of the area and moved across the Strait of Otranto to attack Durazzo, as has already been described, while his brother, Count Roger, began a slow conquest of Muslim Sicily—a conquest which finally was completed, including the island of Malta, in 1090.

Meanwhile, Venice, drawn into the fray, as has been noted, because she opposed Robert's Albanian ambitions, decided to join with Emperor Alexius I of Byzantium in opposing the Guiscards. A short but fierce struggle ensued in 1085 and 1086 in which Robert and his forces were expelled from the Balkans. The Venetians were rewarded for their efforts by being given special trading privileges in Constantinople and much of *Romania*, which was to be the basis of much of their later prosperity. By 1090 Venice, Genoa, Pisa, and Norman Sicily had appeared as powers in the central and western Mediterranean.

Hard on the heels of these events came a further western European maritime expansion eastward in what we know as the First Crusade.

The Norman, northern French, and Provençal armed contingents who made up this expedition reached Syria and Palestine by overland routes, helped along the way by the Byzantine emperor, who used their advance across Anatolia as a screen while he rebuilt his fleet and regained the coastal area of Asia Minor from the Turks. What made possible the Crusaders' ultimate success in Syria and Palestine was in no small measure the fleets which the Genoese and Pisans sent directly by sea to aid them. After Jerusalem had fallen and the formation of the Crusaders' principalities had begun, a process which continued over the next two decades, these same Italians, now joined by the Venetians and by some northern European contingents, helped capture the coastal ports, one after another, and were rewarded by being given special quarters and trading privileges in each of them. From this time on, they shared in a lucrative east-west trade, in which they carried pilgrims east and returned with spices and other eastern wares. The Latin west had established itself as an important naval and maritime power in the Levant, although it shared this position with Byzantium, whose revived navy was strong enough to exclude all but the favored Venetians from the waters of her empire.

During the remainder of the twelfth century, all three Italian maritime powers, along with the Normans in Sicily, continued to expand their influence on the sea, combining, in the process, trading, raiding, and outright war in an unusual way. Pisa and Genoa, for instance, were willing to combine forces for expeditions such as an attack on the Balearics or the seizure of Almeria and Tortosa, though they were more often in conflict with one another. In their attacks upon Iberian or Syrian Muslim ports, they mastered the art of amphibious warfare, while they traded as far west as Morocco and as far east as Alexandria and Acre. First Pisa and then Genoa proceeded to join Venice in a lucrative trade with Constantinople. The Genoese were able to make great profits from the transport of King Philip II's French forces to Palestine during the Third Crusade, and they showed how effectively their crossbowmen, recruited largely in Corsica, could operate from the rigging during naval assaults on hostile shores and fleets.

Though Venice seems to have been, on the whole, more commercially minded than her two western Italian rivals, she too showed she could mix war with trade. Thus, she launched raids in the Aegean which forced a reluctant Emperor John Comnenus to renew the Gold-

en Bull, used force to keep Dalmatia under her overlordship, and
helped Byzantium expel Roger II of Sicily from Corfu and Greece in
1148. In short, while they developed a thriving commerce using the
effective capitalistic *commenda* system of partnership, the Pisans,
Genoese, and Venetians were as concerned with war as a business as
they were with trade, and managed to mingle *both* with a crusading
spirit they shared with the French, Spanish, English, and German
fighting nobles of the period.

The Kingdom of the Two Sicilies followed much the same pattern, especially during the reigns of Roger II (1103–54) and William I
(1154–66), whose fleets dominated the central Mediterranean, worked
closely with the Pisans, Genoese, and Venetians, and for some decades controlled every important Muslim port from Bone to Tripoli.
As late as 1185, the Normans sent a great fleet to seize Saloniki from
the Byzantines, and their state–run economic system anticipated much
that was to be typical of the reigns of Frederick II and later Renaissance princes. Though none of these four Italian maritime powers had
by 1200 wholly taken the place of either Byzantine or Muslim sea
power in the Mediterranean or eliminated their merchants from
lucrative markets, they laid the foundations for doing so in the years
ahead.

Let us now turn our attention to the kinds of ships used by these
Italian mariners. Most traffic was carried on by small ships of various
designs, which generally operated as coasters. Venice's Adriatic commerce, or that of Genoa or Pisa along shores between Sicily and the
Rhone, especially, operated in this manner. Larger vessels, however,
were needed for longer voyages, and two basic types seem to have
been utilized: the so-called *naves* or *nefs*, which were large round-
ships, lateen-rigged, with two masts; and galleys, which were the de-
scendents of Byzantine fast *chelandias* or *galleys* of the tenth century
and which, although they carried lateen-rigged masts, depended in
battle on two banks of oars rowed mainly by citizen sailors, who
could use arms when they closed with enemy vessels at close quarters. In general, the Genoese and Pisans appear to have used more
round–ships than the Venetians, who specialized in galleys in the
Byzantine mode. The Venetians, like the Amalfitans, may have preferred galleys because they were influenced by Muslim ship designs,
perhaps because Venice was located among shallow lagoons, where
large round-ships or *naves* were impractical, while Pisa's and Genoa's

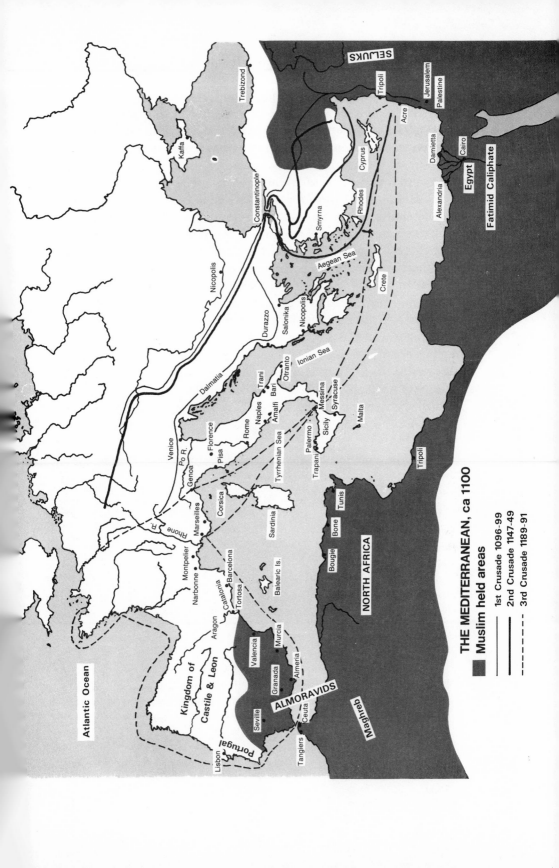

THE MEDITERRANEAN, ca 1100

Muslim held areas

1st Crusade 1096-99
2nd Crusade 1147-49
3rd Crusade 1189-91

SELJUKS

Fatimid Caliphate

Egypt

NORTH AFRICA

ALMORAVIDS

Maghreb

Kingdom of
Castile & Leon

Portugal

Atlantic Ocean

Jerusalem
Palestine
Tripoli
Acre
Damietta
Cairo
Alexandria
Cyprus
Rhodes
Crete
Smyrna
Aegean Sea
Constantinople
Trebizond
Kaffa
Nicopolis
Durazzo
Salonika
Nicopolis
Ionian Sea
Otranto
Bari
Trani
Naples
Amalfi
Messina
Syracuse
Sicily
Palermo
Malta
Trapani
Tripoli
Tunis
Bone
Bougie
Bougie
Ceuta
Tangiers
Almeria
Granada
Seville
Murcia
Valencia
Aragon
Catalonia
Tortosa
Barcelona
Balearic Is.
Lisbon
Narbonne
Montpelier
Marseilles
Rhone R.
Corsica
Sardinia
Tyrrhenian Sea
Pisa
Florence
Rome
Genoa
Venice
Po R.
Dalmatia

deep-water harbors could handle such large vessels much more
easily.

We also need to understand how the Italians used armaments on
their ships. Anna Comnena has left us an account, already noted, of
how Robert Guiscard built large castles covered with hides on his
ships so that they could sail right up to the city walls of Durazzo and
attack them from the sea. And all these vessels were at times armed
with catapults and petries, which could throw large missles at their
enemies on land or at sea. Late in the century, it was the custom to fill
the rigging and crow's nests of warships with crossbowmen, who
could keep up a devastating fire against their opponents, and Greek
fire was in regular use. Since every sailor or oarsman doubled as a
warrior in time of need, we can regard every ship as a potential floating fortress. This versatility helps to explain why these Italian maritime powers were so much more successful than their Byzantine or
Muslim counterparts, whose merchants were always unarmed and
who lacked the warlike mentality of the Italians. No wonder that,
when they were unemployed, Venetian and Genoese seamen so easily turned to piracy during the reigns of the Angeli of Byzantium,

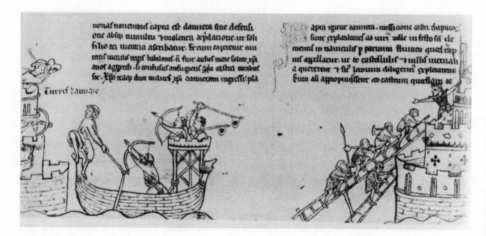

Siege of Damietta of 1219 as illustrated in the thirteenth-century
history by Matthew of Paris. The amphibious operations involved
in the attack are clearly illustrated. Ships could be drawn up close
to the walls and bridged from the decks or by gangways attached to
the masts. By permission of the Masters and Fellows of Corpus
Christi College, Cambridge.

Miniature from Vegetius' treatise *De Re Militari*, composed in
1271. The crossbow is prominently displayed, as is the advantage of
the top castle as a place from which to hurl stones or other objects
on the enemy. Note the use of hooks, not only for grappling. Repro-
duced by permission of the Syndics of the Fitzwilliam Museum,
Cambridge. MS. Marley Add. 1, f. 86.

making the Aegean and Ionian Seas into a lair of pirate craft that operated much like the seventeenth-century buccaneers of the Spanish
Main.

As the thirteenth century dawned, the pattern of naval and maritime power in the Mediterranean began to change once again. Amalfi,
which had been plundered by the Pisans in 1181, ceased to have any
maritime importance, even though the Kingdom of Sicily continued,
during the reigns of Frederick II and his successors, to maintain naval
forces sufficiently powerful to force the Emirs of Tunis to pay regular
tribute, thus making it possible to lower the customs dues charged

Sicilian merchants. Even more important was the development of maritime strength along the shores of the French Mediterranean (the Midi), where first Montpellier and then Narbonne and Marseilles became important naval centers, though as much in conjunction with the Pisans and Genoese as in opposition to them.

These developments were followed by the swift rise of Barcelona and Catalonia to naval importance. King Jaume, as has been noted, added the Balearics and Valencia to his Aragonese realm and developed sizeable fleets and maritime interests by midcentury. Jaume's own account of his first naval expedition to seize the Balearics reveals the naval strength he was able to muster.

> I waited till the fleet was complete. . . . And the fleet was this: there were twenty-five full-sized ships and eighteen *taridas*, and seventeen galleys, and a hundred *brices* and *galliots*; and so there were in all a hundred and fifty large vessels, besides small barques.
>
> And before starting I ordered how the fleet should go: first, that the ship of En Bovet, in which Guillen de Moncada went, should lead, and should carry a lantern as light; and that of En Carrós should take the rearguard, and carry another lantern as light. And that the galleys should go round the fleet, so that if any galley [of the enemy] came to the fleet, it should first encounter our galleys . . . I myself sailed in the rear of the whole fleet on the galley of Montpeslier; and I collected fully a thousand men in boats who wished to go with us. [*The Chronicle of James I, King of Aragon Surnamed the Conqueror*, trans. J. Forster (London, 1883), I, pp. 112–13.]

Following a great defeat at the hands of Genoa in 1284, Pisa lost importance as a maritime power. By the last years of the thirteenth century, this part of the Middle Sea saw the Genoese and the Catalans share naval and maritime leadership, closely followed by the French Midi and by the Kingdom of Sicily.

Even greater changes were taking place in the Levant, caused by the Fourth Crusade of 1202–1204, which destroyed the effective power of the Byzantine Empire and its naval forces for all time. The Crusaders' success is explained in the following eyewitness account of their attack on Constantinople.

> On the Thursday after mid-Lent (8th April 1204), all entered into the vessels, and put their horses into the transports. Each

division had its own ships, and all were ranged side by side; and the ships were separated from the galleys and transports. . . . On the Friday morning the ships and the galleys and the other vessels drew near to the city in due order, and then began an assault most fell and fierce. In many places the pilgrims landed and went up to the walls, and in many places the scaling ladders on the ships approached so close, that those on the towers and on the walls and those on the ladders crossed lances, hand in hand. But for our sins, the pilgrims were repulsed in that assault, and those who had landed from the galleys and transports were driven back into them. . . . And some remained with their ships at anchor so near to the city that from either side they shot at one another with petraries and mangonels. . . .

On the Monday [they agreed] they would return to the assault, and they devised further that the ships that carried the scaling ladders should be bound together, two and two, so that two ships should be [ready] in case [needed] to attack one tower. . . . And two ships that were bound together, of which one was called the *Pilgrim* and the other the *Paradise*, approached so near to a tower, the one on the one side and the other on the other—so as God and the wind drove them—that the ladder of the *Pilgrim* joined on to the tower. . . . When the knights see this, who are in the transports, they land and raise their ladders against the wall, and scale the top of the wall by main force, and so take four of the towers. And all began to leap out of the ships and transports and galleys helter-skelter . . . and they draw horses out of the transports; and the knights mount and ride straight to the quarters of the Emperor. . . . [Geoffrey de Villehardouin, *Chronicle of the Fourth Crusade and the Conquest of Constantinople* in *Memoirs of the Crusades*, trans. F. Marzials (London, 1957), pp. 59–62.]

Venice suddenly gained for herself a maritime empire beyond the Adriatic based upon a series of ports leading into the Aegean, located on Crete, Negreponte, and other islands, and a privileged position in Constantinople, which after 1204 became the seat of a Latin Emperor. Venice now controlled most of maritime *Romania* and the Black Sea as well.

Eager to extend their control over the entire eastern Mediterranean, in 1253 the Venetians proceeded to attack the Genoese in Acre and elsewhere in the Levant. Though they won a number of spectacular victories at sea, they failed to keep the Byzantine Emperor Michael Paleologus from recovering the city of Constantinople in 1261, so that when hostilities ended in 1270 there was no real victor. Venice remained supreme in lower *Romania*, in Cyprus and northern Syria, while Genoa controlled Pera, just across from Constantinople, and the Black Sea. Both operated on equal terms in Egyptian and Palestinian ports.

Meanwhile, another great naval struggle erupted in the western Mediterranean, where Charles of Anjou, the brother of the sainted King Louis IX of France, had made himself ruler of Provence and with Genoese and papal assistance had gone on to take over Naples and Sicily from the heirs of the German emperor, Frederick II. In 1281, however, his Sicilian subjects rose in revolt, and Frederick III of Aragon came to their aid with a large fleet. This ushered in a long war in which the Sicilians and Aragonese fought on land and sea against the forces of the Angevins, the Neapolitans, the Majorcans, and the Papacy. When it ended, the House of Aragon held Sicily and a commanding naval position in the western Mediterranean, while Marseilles had lost its maritime importance. Only Genoa remained as a serious rival to the maritime and naval strength of Aragon in the western portion of the Middle Sea.

While the Angevins and Aragonese were engaged in this struggle, a second Genoese-Venetian naval war took place between 1294 and 1299. This time Genoa won most of the battles at sea, only to have division and conflict at home deprive her of a real victory. So things ended much as they had begun: with the Genoese powerful throughout the entire Mediterranean, but forced to share control of the Levant with the Venetians, and of waters west of Sicily with the Catalans and Provençals.

As competition for dominance in the Mediterranean narrowed down to the Genoese, the Venetians, and the Aragonese, with the Provençals playing a minor maritime role, so many changes took place in these waters that most naval historians have referred to them as the Latin commercial revolution of the thirteenth century. We will not pause to examine the governmental revolution in the west, mentioned in the last chapter, which made available a financial and administrative structure that could support a new naval and maritime level of activity, or economic advances in the use of credit, insurance, and finance, which were even more important. What concerns us here were those special technological and tactical maritime advances which began in this century and were to continue into the next one.

Technological change led to important advances in navigation. By

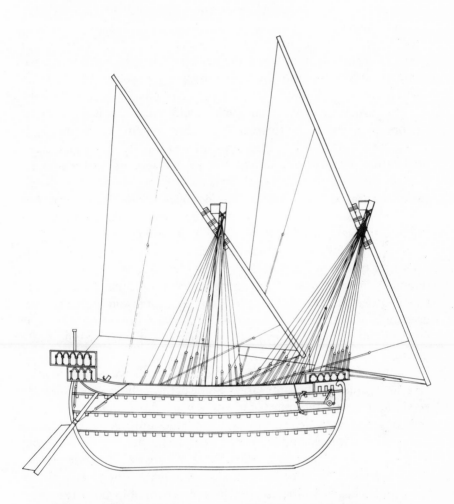

Thirteenth-century Genoese two-masted cargo ship with three decks. This drawing shows a modification of Auguste Jal's Nef X (*Archaeologie navale*, Paris, 1840). The superstructures are taken from the bas-reliefs of two ships on the Leaning Tower of Pisa, and the other elements are based on the research of John H. Pryor. The depth of the hold was estimated at 14'3" (4.34 m.), of the first deck 7'4" (2.33 m.), of the second deck 6'6" (1.98 m.), of the bulwark 4'1" (1.24 m.), for a total depth of about 32'2" (9.79 m.). Earlier reconstructions interpreted this vessel as a two-decked ship. Drawing by John E. Dotson and used by permission of the artist.

the late thirteenth century, the Italian and Catalan mariners had begun to use the boxed compass, which probably originated in northern
Europe, and this use changed the pattern of navigation in the
Mediterranean. It was now possible to extend the sailing time of ships
into the winter season, when the sea had formerly been closed to
navigation, doubling the number of voyages a vessel could make per
year and immensely decreasing shipping costs. It was also now possible to construct portolan charts, which allowed precise navigation in
the open sea. From the thirteenth century onwards these practical
charts for seamen outlined the coastlines of the Mediterranean, and
later of the Atlantic, and provided relative distances between land-
falls. In the later fifteenth century they were based on a latitudinal
scale. Accurate sailing directions across open waters encouraged the
use of more direct routes in place of the longer voyages which followed the coasts, another important cost-cutting procedure.

The state-controlled dockyards such as Venice's Arsenal began to
construct triremes, larger galleys with three tiers of oars, instead of
biremes. These ships were not only faster and more maneuverable in
naval battles but could be built to carry more cargo and could thus be
used for commercial purposes on long convoy runs to the Levant or to
England and Flanders by way of the Strait of Gibraltar, Seville, and
Lisbon.

Commercial round-ships, which were almost always built in private dockyards, also became larger. Some of these ships were enlarged
versions of the old two-masted *naves* or *nefs*, sometimes up to 500 or
600 tons. Others, called *taurides*, were large multiple-masted merchant ships, perhaps originally of Muslim design, used in the western
Mediterranean to carry salt and other bulk cargoes. They may have
been cheaper to build or to operate than a *nef*. About 1300 both of
these types began to be replaced by a northern ship type, the *cog*,
which began to enter the Mediterranean as a new type of cargo vessel.
Jaume of Aragon used cogs in the fleet which attacked Majorca in the
1220s.

The *cog* used a single, large, square sail in place of the lateen rigs of
the *nefs* and the *taurides* and was equipped with a stern rudder instead of with steering oars. Its great advantage over other vessels was
that it could be operated efficiently with much smaller crews than
Mediterranean-type craft, while it could also be built to carry just as
much cargo. Larger round-ships and more efficient *cogs* made pos-

sible continued savings in freight costs for those who used them. The stern rudder also proved so much superior to steering oars that it began to be used by galleys as well as by sailing vessels. And certainly one reason why neither Muslim nor Byzantine naval or maritime power survived in strength to the late thirteenth century is that they failed to make use of any of these new ships or new maritime technological advances.

Equally interesting are the advances in naval tactics. During the twelfth century, major naval battles were few in number. Venice defeated the Fatimid navy in 1128, and Richard the Lion-Hearted scattered Saladin's fleet during the Third Crusade. The latter battle is described in the following account.

> At last on this side of Sidon near Beyrout [Beirut] they descried afar off a certain ship filled with Saladin's choicest warriors.... Richard ... calling one of his galley-men ... bade him row hastily and enquire who commanded it.... It was set off with three masts of great height and its smoothly wrought sides were decked here or there with green and yellow hides.... There was a man present on the king's ship who said he had been at Beyrout when this vessel was loaded. He had seen her cargo sent aboard, to wit, a hundred camel-loads of arms of every kind: great heaps of arbalests, bows, spears, and arrows. It contained also seven Saracen emirs and eight hundred chosen Turks, to say nothing of a great stock of food.... There was also a supply of Greek fire ... and two hundred most deadly serpents [a military device], destined to work havoc among the Christians....
>
> Accordingly at the King's command a galley started after the strange ship at full speed. Seeing this, its sailors [of the Moslem ship] began to hurl arrows and darts against the crew of the galley.... Richard gave the word for an immediate onset. On either side the missles fell like rain and the strange ship now went on at a slower rate, for the oarsmen had to slacken their efforts and there was not much wind. As our galley-men made their circuits round the enemy [ship], they could find no good opportunity of attacking.... Our men ... were grievously bestead by these darts, falling, as they did, from a vessel of such extraordinary height.... Our galley-men... plunged eagerly into the sea and getting under the enemy's ship bound the helm with ropes so as to make the vessel lean to one side and hinder its progress. Others [of our men], pushing alongside ... grasped hold of the cordage and leapt on board.... So the fight continued and warriors fell... till at last the Turks... forced our men back and compelled them to quit the ship....

Meanwhile the king, noting the danger of his men,. . . gave orders for each of his galleys to prick the enemy with its spur [i.e. to ram it with its iron beak]. Accordingly the galleys, after drawing back a space,. . . swept forward under the impulse of many oars to pierce the enemy's sides. By these tactics the ship was stove in at once, and. . . began to sink; while the Turks, to avoid going down with their vessel, leapt overboard into the sea, where they were slain or drowned. The king, however, spared thirty-five of them, to wit the emirs and those skilled in the making of warlike engines. [from *Itinerarium Perigrinorum et Gesta Regis Ricardi*, II, c. 42 in T.A. Archer, *The Crusade of Richard I* (London, 1888), 71–76.]

In the course of the thirteenth century, naval battles became relatively commonplace: for instance, between Venice and Genoa at Acre, Settepozzi and Trapani during their first naval war, which took place between 1258 and 1266. These were followed by Genoa's great defeat of Pisa in 1284 at Meloria and by the battles off Lapazzo and Curzola fought in the second Genoese-Venetian conflict of 1294 to 1299—all of which seem to have taken place on the open sea. And finally we have the naval campaigns waged by Roger Lauria and his Argonese–Sicilian fleet against his French-Angevin opponents at about the same time, especially that naval battle fought in 1282 in the Bay of Naples, in which Charles of Anjou's fleet was destroyed and his son captured. From our perspective, these battles represent the beginning of a modern naval warfare and of the tactics which have decided victory or defeat at sea from this time on.

A surprising skill, which also seems very modern, is evident in the deployment of forces and ships in amphibious operations. The two amphibious assaults that Venetian round-ships and galleys made upon the sea walls of Constantinople during the Fourth Crusade, described above in the eye-witness account of Geoffrey de Villehardouin, resulted in the conquest of the city for the first time in 900 years and were a remarkable accomplishment. They were not to be matched until the present era. Almost as impressive was the amphibious assault on Damietta in the Sixth Crusade, carefully noted by the chronicler Jean de Joinville.

At our left hand landed the Count of Jaffa. . . . It was he who landed in greatest pride, for his galley came all painted, within and without, with escutcheons of his arms. . . . He had at least three hundred rowers in his galley. . . . While he was coming it seemed as if his galley flew, so did the rowers urge it forward with their sweeps. . . . So soon as the galley had been driven into the sand as far up as they could drive it, both he and his knights leapt from the galley, well armed and well equipped, and came and arrayed themselves beside us.

On our right hand, at about a long-crossbow-shot's distance, landed the galley that bore the ensign of St. Denis [the royal French banner]. And there was a Saracen who, when they had landed, came and charged in amongst them, . . . but he was hacked to pieces. [Jean de Joinville, *Chronicle* in *Chronicle of the Crusades*, trans. F. Marzials (Harmondsworth, 1969), pp. 174–175.]

The early development of amphibious tactics in the twelfth century was certainly perfected in this battle.

On the other hand, the course of events during the thirteenth century reveals quite clearly that naval and maritime power had serious limitations as well. When they left sea power behind, the Latin westerners found themselves much less able to operate successfully in the interior. Hence, their inability to defeat the Bulgars and the Greek successor states of the Balkans and Asia Minor after the fall of Constantinople in 1204; their failure to hold Jerusalem for long after they had recovered it in 1229; and their inability to advance successfully up the Nile from Damietta in the course of the Sixth Crusade. Even the loss of the Syrian coastal cities to the Mamluks after 1260 showed that sea power alone could not accomplish everything, unless it was backed up by other forms of military strength. So, if the thirteenth century in the Middle Sea marks the birth of mature, modern naval tactics and amphibious operations, it also highlights the limitations of sea power in dealing with opponents determined to resist and possessed of considerable armed strength upon the land—a lesson which the Americans were to make clear to the British during our Revolution and which the Vietnamese in turn were to make clear to the Americans during the recent conflict in southeast Asia.

Initially, the fourteenth century seems very similar. Naval conflicts continued in both the eastern and western Mediterranean. In the west, the Catalans defeated Genoa and added a restive Sardinia to their maritime empire, while in the east the Venetians and Genoese fought two increasingly destructive naval wars, which finally ended in a draw after Venice had survived an attack upon her lagoons in home waters. Both these wars ended as they did, however, because the Genoese were unable to maintain any unity in their home city.

All these conflicts saw an increasing use of convoys to protect commerce, another seemingly modern practice. Such convoys, which had begun to be used by the Genoese and Venetians even before the First Crusade, became annual affairs, linking the western Mediterranean with the east, especially during periods of conflict. But at the same time, after repelling a Merinid attack upon Spain in 1340, in no small measure through the destruction of their fleet in the Strait of Gibraltar, Latin Europe launched its last successful amphibious operation, an attack upon the Egyptian port of Alexandria which took place in 1365.

Nevertheless, by the last years of the fourteenth century, one begins to sense a slacking off of Latin successes on the sea. The Black Death, which struck western Europe in 1348 and again in the 1360s, had a serious effect upon its maritime operations. Much of Latin Europe felt leaderless when the Papacy was divided by the Great Schism, and French and English monarchies insisted upon using their resources in a long and fruitless Hundred Years War. When the Bardi and Peruzzi banks failed in Florence in midcentury, the financial resources of Europe could not be effectively mustered for commercial purposes as had been the case earlier. Finally, trading cities everywhere, such as Florence, were rent by social conflict and economic decay.

For these reasons, western Europeans after 1365 seem to have acted upon the sea with less confidence, especially in relation to the Islamic world. Piracy increased along North African shores, and Christian militias were replaced by tribal and renegade contingents at the courts of local rulers. A large expedition sent to seize ports in Tunisia in 1390 was beaten off with heavy losses. As we have stated, the Mamluks of Egypt were even able to build a fleet, suppress the independence of Lesser Armenia, and force Cyprus to pay tribute, without being checked by the naval forces of the Latin west.

Finally and most important, the naval power of the westerners—especially that of the Venetians and Genoese—proved unable to stop the expansion of the Ottomans into Europe or into Asia Minor after 1365. Such sea power as existed could temporarily protect Byzantine enclaves at Constantinople, Salonika, or the Morea, but it was unable to play any role in the disastrous defeat of the west at Nicopolis in 1396, which assured the Turks' control of the Balkans.

A ship caught in a storm with the crew appealing to St. Nicholas of Bari, patron of mariners, who comes to the rescue. The crew is jettisoning cargo in order to lighten the vessel the better to ride out the storm. Painting by Bicci di Lorenzo (d. 1452). Ashmolean Museum, Oxford.

In short, although the Latin west continued to perfect its maritime and naval technology by building bigger galleys, by using the cog with its single sail and stern rudder, and by making use of the compass and portolan chart in navigation and in the drawing of accurate maps—and even by beginning to employ cannon on its ships—the fourteenth century ended with the west's maritime strength and naval expertise less effective than had earlier been the case. As a result the Muslim world of the Middle Sea began to recover and regain some confidence in its ability to resist sucessfully.

Perhaps the most important development of the fifteenth century was the continued growth of Venice's maritime empire after a fourteenth-century pause. It not only came to include a considerable area on the Italian mainland, won in a series of bitter struggles with the Milanese, but also extensive possessions in Dalmatia, along the Ionian coasts of Greece, and in the Aegean, and even the vital island of Cyprus. Though many of these possessions were only held temporarily before they fell to the Turks, a considerable number proved more permanent. Although the Genoese were able to maintain some bases in the Black Sea and in the Aegean up to 1460, and were able to fight a brief but bitter war with the Venetians in the 1430s, it was the City of the Lagoons which effectively was the symbol and standard bearer of the Latin west in the Levant during this century, much more than had been the case in the two centuries preceding.

Nor did Venice lack naval and maritime strength elsewhere in the central and western waters of the Middle Sea. Great convoys of her galleys and merchant ships traveled to the salt pans of Tripoli and Ibiza in the Balearics and to Sicilian, western Italian, and southern French ports on their way to Flanders and England. Her fleet of 80 galleys and 300 sailing ships of over 200 tons was certainly the largest in the Mediterranean, and her gold *ducat*, which she was coining at the rate of some 1,000,000 a year, had become the standard currency of this part of the world. Although she now had a serious rival in Ragusa, which took advantage of abundant supplies of ship timber and the produce of interior mines to develop important fleets of her own, the fifteenth century was truly the Imperial Age of Venice in the eastern Mediterranean. A religious pilgrim, Felix Faber, writes as follows of his arrangements for travel back from Alexandria on a Venetian ship in 1483.

> Having finished dinner we went to the Venetian *fonduk* [in Alexandria] and discussed with the captains of the galleys [Venetian] our passage home, the cost, etc. . . . Some of them asked fifty ducats from each pilgrim. . . . Some of the nobles made an agreement with Sebastian Contarini, captain of a galley of the main fleet in which the Consul of Alexandria and his son and the captain of the fleet wished to take passage along with a great number of noble Venetian citizens.
>
> . . . This galley pleased me immensely. It was new, of great size, very well appointed, the crew were pleasant and the captain of the fleet who lived on it was a wise and good man. . . . I ended up being able to travel on this galley and in addition I was given twelve ducats to cover my own expenses in return for which I was to take care of their spiritual needs [as a chaplain]. [From *Le Voyage en Egypte de Felix Fabri, 1483*, ed. and trans. J. Masson (Cairo, 1975), II, pp. 710–712; authors' translation.]

In the west the situation was more complex. Genoa, Venice's old trading and naval rival, managed to make a comeback by the mid-fifteenth century. Her merchants, who were settled in large numbers in overseas centers such as Lisbon, Seville, and Kaffa, were able to use organized, chartered companies such as the Bank of Saint George as a substitute for an effective, urban organization at home. By 1424, as a result, Genoa not only possessed a large number of fighting galleys, but also sixty-three huge, cargo–carrying merchant ships—most of them much larger and more efficient than those of their Venetian rivals. Even more important, though, was the naval and maritime strength of the Aragonese, which, after a late fourteenth-century decline, was now on the rise again, especially after Alfonso V united Naples, Sicily, and Sardinia with his mainland holdings in Valencia, Aragon, and Catalonia. This unity made possible a considerable increase in both the naval strength and maritime prosperity of the House of Aragon after midcentury.

Two new or, rather, renewed maritime powers also appeared in the west. One was Florence, which conquered Pisa in 1406 and used her galleys to link Medici-controlled Tuscany with distant England and Flanders by way of the Strait of Gibraltar. The other was southern France, where fleets of merchantmen were organized by Jacques Coeur in the port of Marseilles to trade with the Levant at the close of the Hundred Years War. Thus, the fifteenth century saw a revival of the maritime strength, moribund for more than a hundred years, of both Pisa and of the French Midi.

The western Mediterranean maritime scene was also distinguished by a new aggressiveness directed against Muslim shores. In 1415 the Portuguese captured Ceuta—a city opposite Gibraltar—which they held onto in the face of constant Moroccan efforts to recover it. In 1471 they were able to add control of Tangiers and of most ports along the Atlantic shore as far as Agadir. As a result they were able to enter the Mediterranean freely and to deny to Muslim enemies ports from which they could harry Portuguese merchant fleets.

While the Portuguese were taking control of Ceuta and Atlantic Morocco, the Castilians were busy on the Mediterranean side of the Strait. In 1462 Gibraltar fell to Castile, and soon thereafter Ferdinand and Isabella, whose union had joined together the resources of Castile and Aragon, launched a great land and sea attack upon Granada. By 1492 Granada had fallen, and the long *Reconquista* had ended in a Christian victory. Then, after Jews and Moors in large numbers began to move across into North Africa to escape persecution, causing, in so doing, increased numbers of corsair attacks upon the sea, the Catholic kings seized Melilla in 1497 as part of a continuing effort to deny to pirates bases from which to operate.

In the Levant the opposite occurred. Here, the Ottoman Turks, following their victories in the Balkans and in Asia Minor and the capture of Constantinople in 1453, as noted earlier, began to threaten Latin western control of eastern waters. Even before this time the Turks had scored some success by capturing Smyrna, Salonika, and Negroponte from the Venetians and by launching pirate raids on Latin Aegean shipping and island holdings. But they still had been unable, as has been noted earlier, to interfere with the structure of Latin sea power in the eastern Mediterranean. After 1453, the Black Sea became Ottoman, and the Genoese and Venetians were expelled from its waters. The Morea was occupied, and new fleets began to be built in dockyards near Constantinople and in the Aegean. Enrolling both Turks and Greeks, who had considerable practical experience, as their crews, the Ottomans suddenly became a serious menace to Venice and to the Latin Mediterranean world in general, despite Papal efforts to preach Crusades against them and Venetian intrigues with their enemies in eastern Anatolia. By 1480 Ottoman sea power had become formidable enough to seize briefly Otranto at the entrance of the Adriatic. In 1487 and in 1495, Turkish corsair captain Kemal Reis carried on piratical operations against the Spanish coastline from ports such as Bougie or Bone or from the island of Gerba in the Maghreb. By 1498 a new era had dawned, in which Latin Europe, which for three centuries had been without serious rivals in Mediterranean and Black Sea waters, suddenly faced the threat of Ottoman sea power—a threat which was to continue for more than a century.

What other changes, besides new Ottoman sea power, distinguished this final medieval century in the Middle Sea? Perhaps one of the more important was in ship types. Already by 1400, as we have noted, the older Mediterranean round-ships such as *nefs* and *taurides* had been replaced by more efficient northern European *cogs*. Two other new ship types began to appear in Atlantic and in Mediterranean waters of the time. One was the *caravel*, a multiple-masted vessel using a combination of square sails and lateens, which by 1436 had been developed by the Portuguese for use in the Atlantic and along the shores of West Africa.

Panorama of the harbor at Naples in a painting by an unknown artist, about 1464–74. The variety of vessels reflects the changes in
ship design at this time. Courtesy of the Museo di Capodimonte,
Naples.

The other and much more important ship type was the *carrack*,
which seems to have been a modification of the *cog*, using carvel
methods of construction, and carrying a number of masts and square
sails. Though the *carrack* seems to have first appeared in the Atlantic
area, unlike the *caravel* it became a Mediterranean vessel, too, and
soon was the most important merchant sailing ship in these waters.
Often built as large as 700 or 1,000 tons, *carracks*, which were sometimes also called *nefs* in the fifteenth century, carried most of the
heavy bulk cargoes, such as salt, wheat, cotton, and timber, throughout the Mediterranean. So effective were they as sailing ships that
they even reduced the dependence upon galleys for the Atlantic run to
Flanders. By the end of the century, they had become the western
sailing ship par excellence in all the waters which surrounded the
European continent.

Finally, we find a growing use of cannon and firearms at
sea, which ended the older dependence upon crossbows and catapults
by crews on merchant ships and galleys as well. Use of such weapons
explains in part the success of the Spanish and Portuguese along the
shores of Morocco and in the final capture of Granada. Skill in the use

Italian engraving of a three-masted carrack, ca 1470–80, one of the finest contemporary representations of a fifteenth-century vessel. National Maritime Museum, Greenwich, England.

of firearms also explains, on the other hand, why the Janissaries were such formidable adversaries and why the Ottoman privateers and galleys were able to oppose the Venetians so successfully in the eastern and central Mediterranean. Although naval tactics had been perfected in many ways in the thirteenth century, and more modern methods of navigation and of carrying on maritime trade had been developed, it was the *carrack*, the musket, and the ship's cannon that finally completed the process and, after 1492 or 1498, launched the peoples of western Europe on their way to a new destiny as masters of the seven seas of the wider world. Ironically, at this same time their Ottoman enemies were about to add Mamluk Egypt and Muslim North Africa to the Ottoman Empire, thereby challenging the Latin west in the Mediterranean and Black seas, a region dominated by the west during most of the period since the millennium.

CHAPTER V

Irish, Frisians, and Vikings in the Northern Seas, 500–1066

BY 500, ABOUT THE TIME the western Roman Empire disappeared from history, northern Europe began to move toward a new naval and maritime destiny. Almost at once, as we have already noted, two rather distinct maritime centers began to emerge in northern waters. The first was a Celtic one stretching from Galicia and Britanny to Ireland, Scotland, and western Britain—a thalassocracy essentially Atlantic in nature.

The second was centered on the North Sea and spilled over into the English Channel, including within it most of eastern England, Frisia, northwestern Germany, and, at times, parts of Denmark and the western entrance into the Baltic. The Celtic thalassocracy to the west was characterized by a large-scale movement of Celtic peoples to the peninsula of Britanny during the two centuries just before and after 500, and in the North Sea area these years were marked by an even more important migration of Jutes, Saxons, and Baltic Angles across the sea into Britain—a migration which, by about 600, had begun to transform the eastern portion of this island into the England of the future.

Each of these migrations of large numbers of people by sea was associated with special kinds of ships. Though the Irish and Celts of western Britain certainly were able by this time to build and use small wooden cargo sailing ships, descended from types which Caesar found in these waters much earlier or from vessels introduced by the Romans from the Mediterranean—vessels which recent excavations in England have revealed to us in some detail—their most important ship was of a quite different type. It was the large seagoing *curraugh*, made of several thicknesses of hides stretched over a wooden or wicker frame, with a mast and a capacity for carrying up to a score of people as its crew, and able to ride like a cork on the waters of the stormy Atlantic and to sail safely over long distances.

The Saxons and Angles who crossed the North Sea to invade and settle in Britain from 450 on seem to have used a type of clinker-built rowing barge without a mast, which could operate along the coast but not very effectively in the open sea. Such craft, developed from the earlier Nydam boat and revealed for us in the Sutton Hoo ship, discovered in Suffolk and dating from circa 630, or even in the more controversial Kvalsund boat from Norway, in use about 700, were the ships which carried the Anglo-Saxons down along the coast of Frisia and then across the North Sea to England. Contemporary ships are described by Procopius, who gained information about them from the Angles who came with Frankish ambassadors to visit Justinian. Surprisingly, they are commanded by a woman.

Then [Radigis, King of the Varni], by the will of the notable men among these barbarians, carried out the counsel of the dead king, and straightway renouncing his marriage with his betrothed, became wedded to his stepmother. But when the betrothed of Radigis [a princess of the Angili in Brittia, probably modern Denmark] learned this, she could not bear the indignity of her position and undertook to secure revenge upon him for his insult to her. For so highly is virtue regarded among these barbarians, that when merely the name of marriage had been mentioned among them, though the fact has not been accomplished, the woman is considered to have lost her maidenhood. First, then, she sent an embassy to him. . . . But since she was unable to accomplish anything . . . she took up the duties of a man and proceeded to deeds of war. . . .

She accordingly collected four hundred ships immediately and put on board them an army of not fewer than one hundred

Model of the Kvalsund ship, ca 700. Length about 59' (18m.), beam
9'10" (3m.). The emergence of a rudimentary keel is found here.
This vessel anticipates the combined oared/sailing ship of the Viking era. Bergens Sjøfartsmuseum, Bergen.

thousand fighting men. . . . And there were no supernumeraries
in this fleet, for all the men rowed with their own hands. Nor do
these islanders have sails, as it happens, but they always navigate
by rowing alone. . . .

Along the coast of the ocean which lies opposite the island of
Brittia there are numerous villages [i.e., Frisia]. These are in-
habited by men who fish with nets or till the soil or carry on a
sea-trade with this island. . . . [and who also have the duty of
ferrying the souls of the dead to Brittia. They are awakened at
night and go to the shore.] There they see skiffs . . . in which they
embark and lay hold of the oars. And they are aware that the
boats are burdened with a large number of passengers . . . but after
rowing a single hour they put in at Brittia. And yet when they
make the voyage in their own skiffs not using sails but rowing,
they with difficulty make this passasge in a night and a day. [Pro-
copius, *History of the Wars*, VIII, xx, 26–31 and 49–55, trans.
H.B. Dewing (Cambridge, Mass., 1953), 259–61, 267–69.]

By the seventh century, however, two quite different North Sea
ship types had made their appearance, the hulk and the cog, both of

which seem to have originated along the coasts of the Netherlands in what today is Belgium and Holland. They were quite different from either the Sutton Hoo or Kvalsund rowing barges. The hulk, the earliest extant example of which dates from the first years of the eighth century, was shaped somewhat like a banana and bore a sail for propulsion. It lacked a keel and was especially adapted for beaching along sandy shores and estuaries at a time when the quays and wharves which the Romans had introduced in these waters had long since disappeared. Its counterpart, the cog, went back to a much earlier second-century prototype and was flatbottomed and tubbier in design than either the earlier rowing barge or the hulk. It too used a sail, had two side oars for rudders and considerable space for cargo. It could not be beached, but was designed to ride onto a sandbank at high tide and then be refloated when the tide came in again. Both ships were ideal small cargo vessels for the sandy estuaries on either shore of the North Sea. A third vessel, the keel, appeared some time in the eighth century along the English coast. This vessel was essentially a keeled Kvalsund boat, which now carried sails and resembled the later Scandinavian trading ship known as the knarr.

In the eighth century, as North Sea migration ceased and the Anglo-Saxons settled down in England, the leading maritime role in this part of the northern seas was assumed by the Frisians, who sailed their cogs and hulks to England and to Atlantic Norway. They also traded with the Baltic port, Hedeby, at the foot of the Danish peninsula and as far north as Birka in Sweden, carrying the products of the Rhineland and of the Carolingian Empire to this northern European world. Small cogs and hulks proved ideal vessels for carrying valuable cargoes to these small *portuses* without wharves, which had by now sprung up along the shores of the North Sea and of the Channel, and into the Baltic from Quentovic and Dorestad to London, York, Hedeby, and Birka.

During this century sea power also developed in the Celtic world. Here small wooden carvel-built sailing ships of Romano-Celtic design sailed along western Gallic and Iberian shores, especially from the mouths of the Garonne and the Loire, carrying cargoes of wine north to exchange for hides and tin and other metals found in the newly converted Christian world about the Irish Sea. Some ships may even have linked this northern world with the western Mediterranean, now controlled by Justinian and his immediate successors.

Even more remarkable, however, was the northward movement of other Irish navigators in skin curraughs to the Shetlands, Orkneys, and out into the Atlantic as far as Iceland. In their wake came monks and others, who settled in some numbers in these islands and who, if we can believe the legendary accounts associated with Saint Brendan, sailed in coracles even further west to Greenland and the coasts of North America.

While Celtic peoples were moving in force to Britanny and then proceeding northward as pioneers to the islands of the northern Atlantic and while Anglo-Saxons were gradually transforming Britain into England, peaceful conditions seem to have prevailed along the northern sealanes. We hear of no pirate fleets operating anywhere, and there is almost no record of conflicts on the sea.

Suddenly, however, and rather dramatically, this peace was broken by the entrance upon the scene of Scandinavian seamen, whom we know as Vikings. Historians believe that several factors lie behind the sudden explosion of energy which helped to produce the Viking Age after 780. Partly, it was the result of an expansion of the population in Denmark, Norway, and Sweden, which caused many Scandinavians to seek homes overseas, while political consolidation by new royal authorities may have driven defeated rivals out to join in the exodus. It was also a response, especially in Denmark, to pressures exerted by an expanding Carolingian Empire. And, in part, it resulted from the development by the ninth century of new, excellent fighting ships, known as *long ships*, which gave Scandinavians a superiority on the sea that their potential rivals could not match. All of these factors combined, then, to produce a new and turbulent era in northern European waters.

Generally speaking, Norwegian Vikings sailed directly west to the Shetland Islands and down past the Hebrides to dominate the waters around Ireland and the Irish Sea and then proceeded on to western Gaul and northwestern Spain—that is to say, they tended to operate in the area of the old Celtic thalassacracy. The Danes, on the other hand, usually sailed along the shores of Frisia and into the English Channel, raiding and dominating much of eastern Britain and the French and English coasts on either side of the Channel. Swedes, however, were most active in the Baltic, crossing to Livonia and following river systems deep into Russia and beyond.

By the late ninth century, several Viking flotillas even entered the

Mediterranean, where their Norwegian and Danish crews plundered western Mediterranean shores, while others, by 870, after occupying the Faroes, followed the Irish example and began to settle in large numbers in Iceland. Some of these Icelanders pressed on a century later to establish two settlements in southwestern Greenland and even attempted in vain to colonize a part of northern Newfoundland.

Throughout the ninth and tenth centuries, Scandinavians not only colonized the Hebrides, Shetlands, and Orkneys, but also set themselves up in port towns which they established along the coasts of Ireland and in Cumberland, across the Irish Sea in western Britain. Others, mainly Danish, having failed to establish a Viking Frisia, invaded England in force between 865 and 878. Though they failed to conquer the Anglo-Saxons, thanks to Alfred the Great's successful resistance to their invasion, they were able to establish themselves in the area of northern and eastern England known as the Danelaw, which the heirs of Alfred were only gradually able to reconquer between 878 and 950. Finally, during this first wave of violent Viking expansion in the west, a band of Vikings led by a Norwegian chief named Rollo in 911 took over an area of France near the mouth of the Seine, which from this time on was to be known as Normandy and which was to be ruled by Rollo's heirs, who became French feudal dukes. While this activity was going on in the west, in the east other Scandinavians, whom we know as Varangians, were moving deep into Russia, raiding as far south as the Persian shores of the Caspian and the Byzantine coasts of the Black Sea, and establishing under their aegis the powerful principality of Kievan Russia. Thus, by the first decades of the tenth century, Vikings, who had begun by raiding distant shores, had settled in large numbers all the way from Russia and the eastern Baltic to the shores of France, Ireland, and England and to distant Iceland and Greenland.

The method of Scandinavian expansion is interesting. They began by raiding. Then, as time went on, they established more permanent bases at the mouths of rivers leading into the interior, whether in Ireland, Frisia, England, or along the Atlantic and Channel coasts of France. In the third stage they brought in wives and children and advanced in force into the interior to a temporary Viking Frisia or Danelaw in England or to a more permanent Normandy or principality of Kiev. In Atlantic island areas like the Hebrides, Shetlands, Orkneys, Iceland, and Greenland, which had little or no native population, they

settled from the first to form permanent Scandinavian colonies overseas.

After this period of successful expansion came a lull, as more
effective government in Anglo-Saxon England, in Ottonian Germany, and on a local level in Ireland and in feudalized France limited
and even reversed Viking overseas expansion while at home, first
Harold Fairhair in Norway and then Harold Bluetooth and Eric Skot-
konung in Denmark and Sweden began to organize effective states
and suppress piratical excesses.

Not until late in the tenth century did Viking activity begin again.
This time, however, it was on a much larger scale and was carried on
by fleets organized by rulers such as Svein and Canute of Denmark, or
by potential rulers such as Olaf Tryggvason or Olaf Haroldson of Norway. It ended with the emergence of the great Danish empire of Canute, which included England, Denmark, Norway, and parts of the
southern Baltic coastline and which lasted until the middle of the
eleventh century. Or we might consider that this last period of Viking
influence lasted on until William the Conqueror invaded England in
1066 or until Magnus Barelegs of Norway failed in his attempt to
conquer Ireland a few decades later. The latter's failure marks the end
of the age of the Vikings.

Turning from this overall view of Viking expansion over three
centuries to details of naval operations, a few comments are in order.
During their first period of expansion Viking raiders met very little
real opposition. It is true that for a few years Charlemagne organized a
small fleet and naval defenses at the eastern entrance to the English
Channel, and his son Louis the Pious did the same on the Atlantic
shores of Aquitaine. But by 830 this resistance had disappeared, and
the Carolingians seemed unable to cope with the Vikings except by
fortifying a few bridges along rivers leading into the interior and by
building a number of ineffective fortresses. Finally, these monarchs,
especially in France, tried to buy off the marauders with *Danegelds*,
but this effort only intensified the Vikings' raiding zeal.

In the British Isles a similar situation held. In Ireland, where Scandinavians first settled in ports along the coast, the native Irish could
muster no effective forces to deal with them on land or on the sea. The
same was true in England until Alfred was at last able to defeat the
Danes in a series of desperate battles, drive them out of London, and
limit their conquests to the Danelaw. Afterward, Alfred's successors

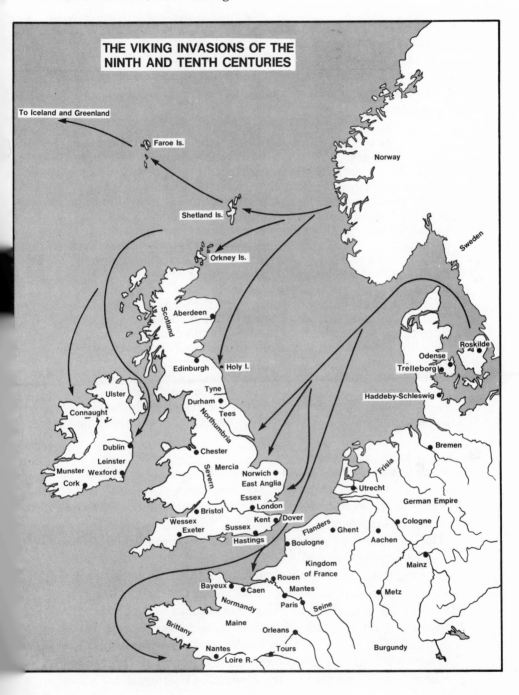

THE VIKING INVASIONS OF THE
NINTH AND TENTH CENTURIES

To Iceland and Greenland

Faroe Is.

Norway

Shetland Is.

Sweden

Orkney Is.

Scotland

Aberdeen

Roskilde

Odense

Edinburgh · Holy I.

Trelleborg

Tyne

Haddeby-Schleswig

Durham · Tees

Ulster

Northumbria

Connaught

Dublin · Chester

Bremen

Leinster

Mercia

Munster Wexford

Severn

Norwich

Frisia

Cork

East Anglia

Utrecht

Essex

German Empire

Bristol

London

Wessex

Kent · Dover

Cologne

Exeter

Sussex

Flanders

Ghent

Aachen

Hastings

Boulogne

Mainz

Kingdom
of France

Rouen

Bayeux · Caen

Mantes

Metz

Normandy

Paris

Seine

Brittany

Maine

Orleans

Nantes

Tours

Burgundy

Loire R.

established fortified *burgs* or boroughs, which helped them gradually reabsorb the Danelaw into an Anglo-Saxon realm. This fortification policy was made even more effective by the building of a fleet and by a naval organization which allowed the English at last to meet the raiders on even terms at sea. The *Anglo-Saxon Chronicle* describes the fleet as follows:

> Then [896] King Alfred had 'long ships' built to oppose the Danish warships. They were almost twice as long as the others. Some had 60 oars, some more. They were both swifter and steadier and also higher than the others. They were built neither on the Frisian nor the Danish pattern, but as it seemed to him himself that they could be most useful. Then on a certain occasion of the same year, six ships came to the Isle of Wight and did great harm there, both in Devon and everywhere along the coast. Then the king ordered (a force) to go thither with nine of the new ships, and they blocked the estuary from the seaward end. Then the Danes went out against them with three ships, and three were on dry land farther up the estuary; the men from them had gone up on land. Then the English captured two of those three ships at the entrance to the estuary, and killed the men, and the one ship escaped. On it also the men were killed except five. These got away because the ships of their opponents ran aground. ... That same summer no fewer than 20 ships, men and all, perished along the south coast. [*The Anglo-Saxon Chronicle*, a revised translation, edited by Dorothy Whitelock with David C. Douglas and Susie I. Tucker (New Brunswick, N.J., 1961), pp. 57–58.]

Though this fleet proved unable to defend England successfully from Svein and Canute's great invasion of 1010–1015, it did show that it was possible to organize an effective naval counterforce to Scandinavian Viking sea power.

During these final years of Viking activity, large battle fleets began to be organized not only by English kings and by their Danish opponents, but also by other Scandinavian rulers in home waters, who used a muster of ships known as *ledings*. Great sea battles took place between such fleets in Norwegian Atlantic waters and in the Baltic as well, often deciding the fate of these rulers and of the realms they ruled. We will describe these battles later on in this chapter. The fleet which William the Conqueror built to transport his Norman and northern French forces across the Channel to Hastings in 1066, like the flotillas which Magnus and Harold Hardrada used to invade Denmark and that which the latter employed to carry his forces across the North Sea to fight his final battle with Harold Godwinson at Stamford Bridge in Yorkshire, were all fleets of this sort. So were the fleets with which Svein Estridson and Canute II menaced England during the last years of William the Conqueror and William II. Then they disappeared as a new era dawned in northern Europe.

The warships which made possible this Viking domination of the northern seas are well known to us, thanks to a number of examples dating to this period from Osberg, Tune, and Gokstad in Norway and from Roskilde in Denmark, of which the Gokstad ship, now completely restored, is the best example. They reveal to us that these *longships*, as they were called, were narrow-keeled, flatbottomed vessels of clinker construction (overlapping planks held together with clinch bolts) which though they had a mast amidships, were in the main propelled by rowers. They had two steering oars, and their shallow draft made it possible for them to navigate up rivers and along coasts with relative ease. Though they could carry up to two score passengers or rowers, they were easy to beach or even portage over short distances using rollers and manpower. The warships which William the Conqueror built for his invasion fleet in 1066, shown in the Bayeux tapestry, were essentially longships.

Quite similar was the Scandinavian merchant ship or *knarr*, of which we also have a number of surviving examples. The *knarr* in its Baltic form was simply a tubbier version of the longship with a deeper draft, keel, and higher freeboard. It was also clinker built and had two steering oars, but it relied upon a large square sail fixed to a single mast for propulsion. It also may have resembled the *keel*, which, as we have noted, was developed somewhat earlier in English North Sea waters. By the tenth century or even earlier, the *knarr* had become the Atlantic and Baltic trading ship par excellence. It was in such ships that Scandinavian colonists sailed west, using advanced navigational techniques, to settle in the Faroes, Iceland, and Greenland.

During that last great age of Viking expansion circa 1000, larger warships came to be built in Scandinavia than the *longships* described above. These were huge, oared vessels of great length and height known as *drekkars* or dragon ships. Unlike the *longships*, they seem to have had high, planked decks, both fore and aft, from which arrows and spears could be rained down on opponents, but they were

The Gokstad ship during excavation in 1880. Universitetets Oldsaksamling, Oslo.

apparently not very maneuverable in battle. Such warships were the
battlewagons celebrated in the sagas which tell of the noble deeds of
leaders such as Svein, Canute, and Olaf Tryggvason. The following
account of the battle of Svolder written by Snorri Sturlson shows how
they could be used in naval combat.

> King Óláf and Earl Sigvaldi had seventy-one ships when they pro-
> ceeded from the south. . . . King Óláf had the trumpets blown for
> all his ships to gather. The king's ship [the *Long Serpent*] was in
> the middle of the battle array, with the *Short Serpent* on one side,
> and the *Crane* on the other. And when they began to lash the
> ships together, stem to stem and stern to stern, they did so also
> with the *Long Serpent* and the *Short Serpent*. . . .

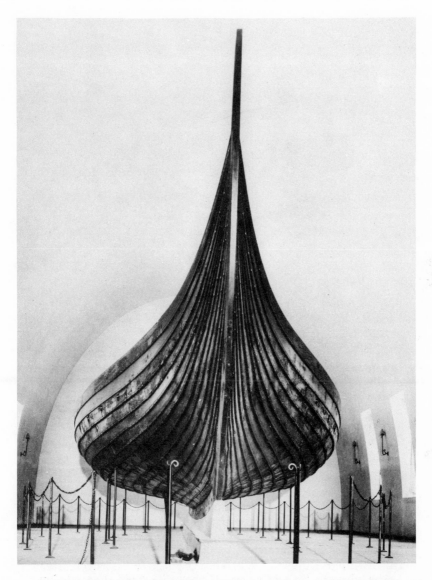

Gokstad ship, ca 850-900. Oak. Length 76½' (23.33 m.), beam 12½' (6.25 m.), height from keel to gunnel amidships 6'5" (1.95 m.). The ship draws 33½" (.85 m.) of water. It is roomy, with loose floor planks to facilitate cargo storage. Viking Ship Museum, Oslo. By permission of the Universitetets Oldsaksamling, Oslo.

View of the reconstructed Gokstad ship from the bow showing her
extraordinarily fine lines. The keel and the clinker construction are
clearly shown. The carved stem and stern pieces with their animal
figures are missing and would have added to the height of the vessel
and its imposing appearance. By permission of the Universitetets
Oldsaksamling, Oslo.

Now the kings [of Denmark and Sweden] rowed to the attack.
King Svein [of Denmark] laid his ship against the *Long Serpent*,
but king Óláf of Sweden from the outside pushed his prows
against the outermost ship of king Olaf Tryggvason from the sea
side while Earl Eirík did so on the opposite side. . . . Earl Sigvaldi
moved his ships to and fro and did not participate in the battle. . . .
Now Earl Eirík brought his ship *Barthi* alongside the outermost ship of King Óláf, cleared it of its crew, and straightway
cut the hawsers connecting it with the other ships, then attacked
the ship next to it, and fought till that was cleared too . . . and in
the end all ships of King Óláf's were cleared of men, excepting the
Long Serpent. . . . There was such a shower of weapons directed
against the *Serpent* that the men could hardly protect themselves
. . . because battleships attacked the *Serpent* on all sides. . . . And
because so great a host of the earl's men had come aboard the

The mast of the Gokstad ship was anchored by a powerful block of oak serving as a keelson and the mast-partner (shown here), which was over 16' long and 3' wide. Note the oar-holes with rounded shutters, which could be closed to seal off the hull. The floor planking was removable for storage of cargo below deck. By permission of the Universitetets Oldsaksamling, Oslo.

Serpent ... and there was but a small band of defenders against so many, ... most were cut down in a short while. But both King Óláf himself and Kolbjorn [his Marshal] leapt overboard, each on his side. [*The Saga of Óláf Tryggvason*, ch. 100–111 in Snorri Sturlson, *Heimskringla*, trans. L. Hollander (Austin, Texas, 1964), pp. 231–241.]

Though Scandinavian ships dominated the waters of the north during the Viking era, they were not the only vessels in use. Off the coast of Aquitaine, carvel-built Atlantic *barcas*, descendants of the wooden vessels of the Irish and ancestors of the *barges* of the High Middle Ages, continued to be built. Large *cogs* and *hulks* also con-

The Oseberg ship partially excavated in Norway, 1904. The Oseberg, Gokstad, and Tune ships were well preserved because of their burial in blue clay. By permission of the Universitetets Oldsaksamling, Oslo.

tinued in use by the enterprising Frisians in navigating and trading about the North Sea and in Scandinavian waters. It is even possible that a larger and tubbier Scandinavian merchant ship known as the *buza* or *buss* had begun to be constructed by the early eleventh century. English rulers, starting with Alfred the Great, built huge rowing galleys, which were perhaps modeled on those of the Mediterranean and which they used with some success against Viking pirate fleets in the narrow seas about Britain. Though from 780 to 1066 Scandinavian-type vessels were the dominant ones used in the northern seas, they were not the only ones that were to be found. Below the veneer of Viking nautical domination, Celtic Atlantic *barcas*, English *keels*, and Netherlandish *cogs* and *hulks* continued in use and to them, as we will show, the future belonged.

The pattern of naval and maritime change about the northern seas

Oseberg ship, ca 800. Oak. Length 71 1/2' (21.33 m.), beam 17' (5.10 m.). This Viking ship was powered by fifteen pairs of oars and a square sail on a single mast. It was not as sturdily constructed as the Gokstad ship, but it is highly decorated in the fashion of the "dragon ships" of this era. Viking Ship Museum, Oslo. By permission of the Universitetets Oldsaksamling, Oslo.

of Europe during this era had economic aspects which must be considered as well. The collapse of the western Roman Empire in the fifth century had an initial effect of bringing to a standstill the trade and commerce that their activities had fostered in northern European waters. Towns disappeared and ports facing the sea in Gaul, Britain, and the Low Countries fell into decay. None of them seem to have been stimulated by the major activity which took place on the sea during the fifth and sixth centuries: the movement of large numbers of people from western British shores to Brittany in the Atlantic or into England from lands across the North Sea. And neither the rowing barges used in the North Sea nor the *curraughs* of the Celts could be used for much more than the transport of people.

Excavation work behind the coffer dam at Roskilde Fjord. Pieces of
the ships were placed in plastic bags and transported to assembly
points for conservation and reconstruction. Viking Ship Museum,
Roskilde, Denmark. Courtesy of Ole Crumlin-Pedersen.

As the Carolingian Empire began to organize itself more effectively during the reigns of Pepin the Short and Charlemagne, and as England did the same under the leadership of Offa of Mercia and Egbert
of Wessex, things began to change. This period was the age of the Frisians, whose traffic in *cogs* and *hulks* linked England and Scandinavia
economically with the Carolingian world, and when small trading
centers or *portuses* reappeared along North Sea and Channel shores.
On a smaller scale, the same thing happened along the coasts surrounding the Irish Sea, which were linked to Aquitaine and distant
Galicia by Celtic maritime activity.

The first Viking raids initially, down to the middle of the ninth
century, put an end to much of this commerce, especially since un-
defended monasteries and *portuses*, the major centers in which
wealth was concentrated, were the places which the Vikings preferred to raid, sometimes repeatedly. But gradually the situation improved. Though Vikings raided, they also traded, especially after they
had established permanent encampments at the mouths of rivers. In

A *knarr* or deep-sea trader, ca 1000, one of five ships found in 1957 at Roskilde Fjord, near Skuldelev, Denmark, and reconstructed. She was 54' x 16' (16.3 m. × 4.5 m.) and built of pine with heavy oak frames, probably in southern Norway. This type of ship was used to carry men and goods to Greenland and America. Viking Ship Museum, Roskilde.

This smaller merchant ship from Skuldelev measures 45' (13.8m.)
×11' (3.4 m.). It was built ca 1000 to sail the Baltic and Northseas
and their tributaries. A single mast supported a square sail. There
are five oar-holes in the forward section and two aft. A steering oar
on the starboard side guided the vessel. Viking Ship Museum,
Roskilde.

Ireland, for instance, many of these encampments, such as Dublin,
Wexford, Waterford, and Cork, soon became permanent towns. As
early as 864, Charles the Bald of France in the Edict of Pîtres found it
necessary to forbid his subjects to trade with Viking pirates, and
Alfred in his well-known peace treaty with Gudrum in 878 did so as
well. Large *Danegelds* paid to Scandinavian raiders also probably increased their trading activities. The silver bullion was used to mint
coins at York or elsewhere. The coins were exchanged for services and
goods, including the maintenance of the army and ships. The Cuer-
dale hoard of 7,000 coins dating to about 900 was found in Lancashire,
England and may be representative of Viking trade activity.

By the tenth century, or even earlier if we can believe Alfred's
Orosius, which tells of trading voyages to Norway and into the distant Baltic, the area of Viking dominance had been transformed into a
huge trading complex which linked Muslim central Asia and Byzan-

Interior view of the smaller merchant ship (Wreck 3) from Skulde-lev. The oar-holes are visible. A prow is mounted on the wall behind the ship.

tium by way of Kievan Russia, with northern Spain, Ireland, and Iceland in the Atlantic. Muslim silver coins from Saminid Iran flooded into the Baltic and are found as far west as Iceland and the British Isles, while Anglo-Saxon and Ottonian silver pennies reached the Baltic in about the same volume. A huge, new, northern seas trading area had been created by Scandinavians on both a peaceful and a warlike level.

As a result, by the tenth century the number of mints and *portuses*, which had begun to appear in Charlemagne's time, quadrupled, aided also by continued agricultural progress and manufacturing development which was transforming that part of Europe which faced the northern seas, especially England, northwestern Germany, the Low Countries, and Scandinavia. Although none of these *portuses* was large (London, with some 15,000 inhabitants probably being the most important), they surpassed in both size and number the urban centers of Roman times. And geographically, they were distributed much more widely, for now there were towns in Ireland, Livonia, and Russia which had not existed at all during the period

A small warship (Wreck 5) found at Skuldelev that resembles those depicted on the Bayeux Tapestry. Rated a *longship*, she was 56' (17.4 m.) × 8 1/2' (2.6 m.) and 3 1/2' (1.1 m.) high amidships. Powered by twelve pairs of oars and a square sail, she was capable of carrying and landing horses on open beaches. Viking Ship Museum, Roskilde.

when the Roman Empire was the strongest economic and maritime power in northern Europe.

The products, other than passengers, which were carried on merchant ships were, as earlier, mainly high-value, nonbulk items such as cloth from Ireland, Britain, and the Netherlands; metal products from a number of regions, such as Rhinelands swords; Baltic furs; and Oriental silks and spices. Occasionally, however, by the tenth century, we hear of bulk products being shipped along the seaways, such as wine from western France and the Rhinelands being sent to newly converted Christians in the north, who needed it for their church services, or English wheat being exported to Scandinavia in return for fish, or honey from Poland.

The shipment of bulk items had a number of important consequences. Since goods carried by sea increased in volume, it paid to construct larger ships, especially efficient cargo carriers such as the

The replicas *Skinfoxe* (a Viking ship) and *Rana* (a type of boat built in northern Norway until about 1900), sailing in a stiff breeze. Tests with replicas have demonstrated the seaworthiness of the vessels. National Maritime Museum, Roskilde. Courtesy of Ole Crumlin-Pedersen.

cogs and *hulks* of the Frisians, the *keels* of the English, or the *busses* of Scandinavia. Such vessels could be more efficiently loaded or unloaded while docked at wharves or quays, instead of beached on sandbars and strands, so we find that in more important ports wooden wharves began to be built. The more effective governments of the period began to suppress pirates, who interfered with the commerce that brought them wealth. Canute of England even organized a standing navy to patrol the seaways dominated by his Anglo-Danish Empire. Christianity, which was now spreading rapidly into pagan Scandinavia and among Scandinavians settled in Iceland, Normandy, and the British Isles, joined Viking society to that of the western Latin world, which looked to Papal Rome for direction and leadership. By 1066 the religious, cultural, and economic world of northern Europe had expanded, making Constantinople, or Micklegrad or Tsargrad as it was called, familiar to Anglo-Saxon nobles and Icelandic adventurers and able to lure Canute to Rome as a pilgrim.

How can one compare this burgeoning Europe, which by 1066 surrounded the northern seas, with that Mediterranean world of Byzantium, Islam, and the new, expanding cities of Venice, Amalfi, Genoa, and Pisa? The former, of course, was much more backward. No cities comparable to metropolitan Constantinople or Antioch, Alexandria, Tunis, or Palermo faced the northern seas, and the volume of commerce and the level of business practices were far behind those found in lands surrounding the Middle Sea. For example, in the north we find nothing resembling the sophisticated business partnerships that Goitein has discovered by examining Geniza documentation, or the *commenda*-like arrangements of Italy or the Byzantine Empire. Only England, which was relatively precocious, had an effective governmental system that organized its law, administration, coinage, taxation, and armed services on a uniform basis. The rest of northern Europe lagged far behind the Mediterranean, and so it was to remain until the time of the Crusades.

On the other hand, we must emphasize the maritime vitality of northern Europe during this period. It had developed in its *curraughs* and Viking *knarrs* ships capable of long oceanic voyages across the stormy Atlantic to settle Europe's first overseas colonies in the Faroes, Iceland, and Greenland. It had the navigational skills, which some have claimed involved the use of sun stones and lode stones, to link these colonies with the European mainland and the British Isles on a regular basis. It had begun to lay the basis for northern Atlantic dominance.

The *cogs, hulks,* and *keels* of the North Sea and the *busses* of Scandinavia, on the other hand, were merchant ships suitable for operation in the narrow seas about Britain and in the Baltic. Northern Europe's seamen also developed a set of sailing directions and navigational skills which were to make possible the new economic development of the lands surrounding northern waters all the way to distant Russia. Already navigational techniques, maritime business enterprise, and technological progress had begun to surpass what Rome had introduced to this part of the world centuries earlier. Remarkably, except for a brief period in the sixth and seventh centuries, when it was possible to sail past Gibraltar to Cornwall and Ireland and back, all this transformation took place in a world which was completely separate from the Mediterranean, except for occasional Viking incursions into southern waters in the eleventh century of permanent significance.

This separation between these two maritime areas explains in no small measure the naval backwardness of northern Europe during the eleventh century. As we have already made very clear, between 500 and 780 northern Europe appears to have had no organized fleets or systems of naval defense at all. Even afterward, except for a brief two decades, during which the Carolingians maintained a flotilla in the Straits of Dover and built shore defenses to ward off Viking attacks, the Scandinavian raiders had no need to worry about either effective shore defense or naval opposition on the high seas.

This situation began to change only when Alfred the Great, late in his reign, was able to obtain financial support throughout England and began to build a fleet and a system of naval defenses for his realm. His successors continued to develop this naval system down to the time of Canute, under whom it probably reached a very high state of efficiency.

It was probably this English example which caused the rulers of first Norway and then Denmark and Sweden to organize a system of mustering ships to defend their realms from attack and which seems to have remained in effect down to the end of the eleventh century and beyond. It was probably also the English decision to build large warships in Alfred's time which caused them to construct those huge *drekkars*, already described, capable of carrying up to 400 men into battle.

Despite these developments, however, there is little evidence that northern European seamen during the early medieval period ever developed any special tactical skills of the sort we find in the Mediterranean. No special amphibious tactics developed other than the simple beaching of warships on a strand. We find no evidence of a special class of scouting ships that differed from other warships. Even the differences between *longships* and supply ships were relatively minor ones, judging from the Bayeux tapestry. The archeological evidence indicates significant differences, but that record remains incomplete.

In naval battles (for which we have no evidence before the tenth and eleventh centuries), ships simply moved into combat with little formation, as has been noted above, and then fought it out individually, using boarding tactics which emphasized that the vessels were simply fighting platforms and little else. We find nothing like the catapults, grappling hooks, or Greek fire of the Mediterranean world used by northern European seamen, who instead relied on bows and arrows, spears, swords, and axes to deal with their naval opponents. In short, until 1066, northern sea power was still not employed tactically or strategically in any way comparable to the employment of sea power in the Mediterranean world of Byzantium and the Islamic peoples.

CHAPTER VI

The Age of the English and the Hansa in the North, 1066–1377

WHEN WILLIAM OF NORMANDY led his northern French knights to victory at Hastings and then went on to crush all resistance to his rule in Anglo-Saxon England, he ended the age of the Vikings in the northern seas of Europe and inaugurated a new era, which was to last down to the final quarter of the fourteenth century. During the three centuries following 1066, England became, along with her dependencies, which she gradually absorbed on the French mainland and in the Welsh, Scottish, and Irish areas of the British Isles, the principal naval and maritime power in the northern seas. She did, however, find that at times during the first two of these centuries, she had to share some of this power with the revived Scandinavian realms of Norway and Denmark and, during the final century, with the even more vital, growing maritime strength of the German Hansa. But until the rise of Iberian sea power toward the middle of the fourteenth century, it was England that was the undoubted naval and maritime leader, succeeding Irish, Frisian, and Viking Scandinavians upon the northern European scene.

Contrary to much historical opinion, however, the development

111

of this Anglo-French Empire, which had such a great maritime significance, was a rather slow affair. It took William the Conqueror most
of his reign to pacify England and to brutally crush resistance in Yorkshire and Northumbria in the face of Danish and Flemish opposition
on the sea and Capetian interference in Norman affairs. His son and
immediate heir, William Rufus, was able to keep control over Normandy, despite his brother Robert, and to extend his dominion over
southern Wales after it had been invaded by his marcher lords.

Only under William's youngest son, Henry I (1100–1135), though,
do we have evidence of real success both on the continent and in the
British Isles. Henry was able to establish overlordship over all of
Wales, integrate northern England into his realm, and, as Norman
lords moved in force into Scotland, get its king to accept his suzerainty. He was equally successful on the continent: he brought effective
government to Normandy; Britanny came under his influence; Flanders accepted an English alliance; and his daughter Matilda cemented
relations with Germany by marrying the Emperor Henry V.

After an interlude under Stephen, the final extension into what
has been rightly called an empire took place during the reign of Henry
I's grandson, Henry II (1153–1189), who not only added Anjou, Maine,
and Eleanor of Aquitaine's French lands to his dominion, thereby be-
coming the direct ruler of two-thirds of France, but also managed to
extend his authority across the Irish Sea into Ireland, which was being
conquered by his Norman Welsh vassals, thereby making himself the
suzerain of the whole of the British Isles. Nor did Henry content himself with these achievements. Relations with Flanders remained
close, despite Capetian intrigues, and the marriage of a daughter to
Henry, the Lion of Saxony, safeguarded England's interests in north
Germany and in the Baltic, just as the wedding of another daughter to
Alfonso VII of Castile did the same in Christian Iberia, which was
steadily expanding south at the expense of the Moors. Despite constant troubles with rebellious sons and with his strong-willed wife,
Eleanor, Henry II a century after Hastings had managed to complete
the development of an empire and sphere of influence which dominated the northern seas from Christian Spain to the Baltic and which
had no serious maritime rivals.

During this century of Anglo-Norman and Angevin successes,
however, the rulers of England never felt it necessary to organize or
maintain a well-defined naval establishment. For instance, though

Shipbuilding shown in the Bayeux Tapestry, late eleventh century
Carpenters are busy constructing ships to carry men, horses, and
supplies for the invasion of England. By special permission of the
City of Bayeux.

William I took over the Anglo-Saxon naval defense system and maintained it, as he did its militia system in general, there is little evidence
that it survived beyond the reign of his son William Rufus, who died
in 1100. By the reign of Henry II, though a royal flagship seems to have
been maintained in the Channel and though both he and his predecessor, Henry I, regularly impressed merchant ships into temporary flotillas to carry their troops across the narrow seas to northern
France, the only organized naval forces regularly available were those
of the *Cinque Ports*, which could be called out for fifteen days of feudal service a year at the king's pleasure.

Perhaps the main reason why English monarchs maintained no
really well-organized naval forces during these years and why they
allowed the old Anglo-Saxon system to disappear was that they feared
no maritime rivals in the northern seas of Europe. In Scandinavia
after 1100, Danish kings had allowed their naval system to decay as
they lost control of their realm to dissident nobles and churchmen,
and southern Baltic shores from Hedeby to the Gulf of Finland fell
prey to piracy. After Norway's last effective Viking ruler, Magnus
Barelegs, died in 1102, his quarreling heirs attempted to rule jointly
with little success, while Sweden likewise lacked regular order. In
short, for most of the twelfth century no effective Scandinavian naval
presence was available in Baltic and North Sea waters. Even in Flanders the naval forces which Count Robert the Frisian was able to

Scene from the Bayeux Tapestry showing the Norman transport vessels used in William of Normandy's invasion of 1066. The steering oar and some of the lines used to support the single square sail are clearly shown. Oar-holes and clinker construction are also indicated. By special permission of the City of Bayeux.

organize briefly about 1080 were allowed to disappear under his successors, despite the growing importance of the sea to rising urban centers and ports such as Bruges and Ghent. If English monarchs maintained no organized naval establishment to hold together their empire during these years, it was because they did not need one.

Nevertheless, considerable *potential* naval power existed about the northern seas of Europe during this period, power which could be mustered, if needed, for maritime enterprise. For instance, we know that soon after 1066, a number of Anglo-Saxon noblemen who were fleeing the English realm, and also Robert the Frisian, sailed south around Spain and past Gilbraltar to reach the Byzantine Empire. A few years later, King Sigurd of Norway, using sailing directions from Viking times, gathered together an even larger armada and followed this same route through the straits to reach Palestine and help King Baldwin I of Jerusalem during the First Crusade.

Wall painting (late fourteenth century) from Skanstrup Church, Denmark, of a Viking-age ship transporting the sainted King Olaf across the seas. Nationalmuseet, Copenhagen.

Still later on, during the Second Crusade, another large joint North Sea force of English, Flemish, and German Bremeners sailed south to assist the Portuguese king, Alfonso Henriques, in his capture of the city of Lisbon, and at about the same time a saga tells of how one jarl of the Orkneys led a small Scandinavian flotilla into the Mediterranean as far as the port of Narbonne. Even though northern European sea power was not yet sufficiently organized to challenge the Norman and Angevin rulers of England, it could muster sufficient maritime strength to capture cities in Iberia and to sail all the way to the eastern Mediterranean. Similarly, Richard the Lion-Hearted was able to organize a large fleet in English and continental ports of his empire, including some Danish and Low Country contingents, and send it through the Strait of Gibraltar during the Third Crusade. This

fleet met him in Sicily, helped him conquer Cyprus, destroyed Saladin's Egyptian fleet off Palestine, and helped support his amphibious
operations along the coast of the Holy Land. This expedition thus
shows what a powerful English ruler could do with northern ships in a
theater of operations which was several hundred miles from his home
ports. The following excerpt from a contemporary chronicler describes the organization of Richard's fleet.

> The fleet of Richard, king of the English, sailed on the open sea
> [on 10 April 1191] and proceeded in this order. In the first rank
> went only three ships, in one of which were the queen of Sicily
> and the Navarrese maiden, perhaps still a virgin. In the other two
> was a part of the king's treasure and arms. In each of the three
> were armed men and victuals. In the second rank there were 13
> ships and busses and dromonds.
>   In the third were 14; in the fourth, 20; in the fifth, 30; in the
> sixth, 40; in the seventh, 60.
>   In the very last one the king himself followed with his galleys.
> Between the ships and their ranks there was such care in the
> spacing of the fleet that from one rank to another the sound of a
> trumpet could be heard, and from one ship to another the voice of
> a man. [*The Chronicle of Richard of Devizes of the Time of King
> Richard the First*, ed. and trans. John T. Appleby (Edinburgh,
> 1963), p. 35.]

By the second half of the twelfth century, northern Europe, whose
English kings could already organize crusading fleets such as that described above, finally began to develop considerable maritime
strength in areas which the Angevin kings of England could not control. One such region was Norway, whose kings, beginning with Olaf
Kyrre and ending with Haakon Haakonson, reorganized the legal and
administrative system and again made the crown an important factor
both at home and in overseas areas such as the Orkneys, Iceland, and
Greenland. Thanks to such rulers, Norway's commerce revived prosperity in towns such as Oslo and Bergen, and the old, fleet *leding*
system was reinstituted. We even hear of the rebuilding of huge *drekkars* or dragon ships between 1182 and 1263, which had been last
used in sea battles at Lags off Scotland toward the middle of the thirteenth century.

Equally significant was the development of new naval and maritime strength, as already noted, in Bremen, Hamburg, and especially
in the Baltic, where the new port of Lübeck assumed importance as

Saxon dukes began to expand their authority into Slavic lands between the Elbe and the Oder rivers. By the end of the twelfth century,
Lübeck had become the most important trading city in this area, exploiting nearby herring fisheries, sending its merchants east to Wendish and Livonian ports and even to distant Russian Novgorod by way
of Visby on the island of Gotland. Thus the foundations of what was
later to become the Hanseatic League were laid.

At the same time, a revived Danish monarchy controlled by the
Waldemars reorganized Denmark's fleet system of the Viking period
and began to expand from its new commercial center of Copenhagen
along the same North Sea and Baltic coasts which were being visited
by German merchants from Lübeck. By the time John Lackland succeeded his brother Richard to become king of England in 1199,
Norwegians, Danes, northern Germans, and Netherlanders had all
developed considerable maritime strength of their own. And so too

Model of a thirteenth-century ship excavated in 1933–34 from the
medieval harbor at Kalmar, Sweden. This coastal vessel has fore and
aft decks separated by a central hold. The straight sternpost is fitted
with a hinged rudder—an important development. The original ship
was 36' (11 m.) long with a breadth of 15' (4.6 m.) and built of oak.
Bergens Sjøfartsmuseum, Bergen.

Cross-section of the "Bryggen Ship" found in excavations at Bergen,
Norway. No fragments of this great ship remain save this cross-
member with maststep. Built of pine, her length was estimated at
90' with a 30' beam. Bryggens Museum, Bergen.

had Angevin ports in France from Normandy to the new, rising wine
port of La Rochelle, which began to assume importance in just this
period.

Then an event occurred which was to have a long-term effect on
the maritime and naval development of northern Europe—the loss by
John of all his northern French lands to Philip Augustus between
1204 and 1215. Suddenly this unlucky Angevin ruler found himself
facing hostile shores across the Channel which soon teemed with
privateers and pirates ready to prey on the commerce of his English
and Gascon subjects. And in Philip Augustus, he found he had an
adversary ever ready to exploit his weakness at home and his troubles
with his barons and his Church by preparing to launch an invasion of
England itself.

Faced by these dangers, John began during his reign to reestablish an effective navy and a new naval defense system. He built a score of royal galleys in shipyards along the coast from Plymouth to the west. He regularized the way in which the Cinque Ports contributed fifty-seven vessels to the king in time of emergency. And he appears to have set up an effective system of pressing into royal service in time of emergency vessels belonging to English or foreign merchants—the beginning of a regular *prize of ships*. He also organized a regular naval administration to maintain, equip, and pay for such fleets and seems to have set up three separate naval and defense commands—one for the Channel, one for the North Sea, and one for western Britain.

John's naval organization proved effective in dealing with privateers in the Channel such as Eustace the Monk, and in 1213 his fleet was able to destroy the flotilla which Philip Augustus had assembled at Damme to invade England itself. In 1216 one of his admirals was able to decimate a second French fleet in a battle fought on the open sea off Dover. Owing something perhaps to tactics and practices learned by English mariners in the Mediterranean during the Crusades, as well as to the contemporary maritime development of Norse and Danish neighbors, English kings had at their disposal at last a real fleet for England and for overseas dependencies in Gascony and Ireland.

Since Philip Augustus's immediate successors were too busy expanding into southern France or going on crusades to challenge the English on the sea, Henry III was able to maintain and perfect the naval establishment set up by his father and to keep active maritime connections with his overseas possessions and his North Sea neighbors—despite his failure to regain lost lands in northern France and constant baronial opposition at home. By 1272 England's position as the leading northern European naval and maritime power remained unchallenged in any serious way.

While John and Henry III were organizing this effective naval establishment in Britain, German trade expanded steadily in the Baltic, and Lübeck continued to serve as a base for traders and crusaders, who organized fleets to sail eastward to Livonia, where they wrested the land from the control of its native inhabitants and organized it into a territory controlled by the Knights of the Sword. This process was also going on in nearby Prussia, where the Teutonic Knights were doing much the same thing. The following account reveals how German crusaders dealt with native sea power.

During the bishop's twelfth year [1210], ... the Kurs, enemies of
Christ's name, suddenly appeared with eight pirate ships off the
shore of Sunde. When they saw them, the pilgrims [Crusaders]
left their cogs, entered smaller boats, and hurried to the pagans.
With insufficient caution, each boat went ahead ... to meet the
foe first. Then the Kurs, by unloading the fore parts of their pirate
ships, raised them up to meet those who were coming, arranged
them two by two, and at the same time left a space between each
of the pairs. For this reason the pilgrims who came on first in the
two skiffs, or small boats, were trapped in the space between the
pirate ships and, because they were in small boats, were not able
to get at the enemy who stood high above them. When some of
them had been killed by the enemies' lances, some drowned, and
some wounded, the others returned to the larger ships and escaped. [*The Chronicle of Henry of Livonia*, trans. J.S. Brundage
(Madison, 1961), pp. 94–95.]

   These two Crusading orders, soon bound together, were aided by
the Danish monarchy and its nobles, which also sent out expeditions
to establish an overseas dominion in Estonia, and by Sweden, which
began a slow, steady penetration of pagan Finland. As a result, the
southern and eastern shores of the Baltic were transformed into areas
controlled by the Teutonic Knights and other nobles, while the
growth of German towns along Wendish and Livonian shores under
Lübeck's leadership led to the formation of the Hanseatic League.

   At the same time, maritime changes of even greater significance
were occurring in the Iberian Peninsula. Here in 1217 the Portuguese,
aided by a crusading fleet on its way to the Holy Land, finally captured
the main advance Muslim naval base of Alcacer do Sol. Some three
decades later in 1248, the Castilians, after they had driven south and
captured Andalusia from the Moors, were able with Genoese, Catalan, and northern Spanish naval assistance to seize the great naval
arsenal at Seville and, after capturing Cadiz in 1262, to get control of
the Strait of Gibraltar at last. In so doing, they established a navy of
their own, manned by the northern Spanish of their Cantabrian and
Basque coasts and employing the skill of a number of Genoese seamen, whom they hired as admirals. Soon thereafter their Portuguese
neighbors, who had completed the conquest of the Algarve, established their own navy. Thus by 1272 in both Castile and Portugal,
which together form the southern Atlantic edge of the northern seas,
newly organized naval forces capable of dealing with ships from

northern Europe entering and leaving the Mediterranean had appeared.

Such traffic was not negligible during the first three quarters of the thirteenth century. It began when the Countess of Flanders led a Netherlands fleet from the North Sea past Gibraltar and on to Palestine during the course of the Fourth Crusade. It continued when another large northern flotilla sailed in 1217 to Damietta to join in the Fifth Crusade, and again when northern ships sailed directly to Egypt at the time of Saint Louis IX's Sixth Crusade, and when, a few years later in 1267, others joined the future Edward I in his futile expedition to the Holy Land just prior to his accession to the English throne. By the late thirteenth century, as we have noted, the northern European compass and the cog, with its useful rudder for steering, were known in the Mediterranean and adopted by Italian, Provençal, and Catalan mariners, in no small measure due to the arrival of northern ships there in large numbers, as outlined above.

The situation changed rather suddenly in northern Europe when Philip (IV) the Fair became king of France in 1285 and began a long struggle with Edward I of England, a struggle with important naval and maritime consequences. Philip was concerned with asserting his royal authority in both Flanders and Aquitaine, which owed him feudal suzerainty. Edward I had important interests in both, since Flanders was England's most important outlet for her wool and since Aquitaine was not only ruled directly by Edward as duke, but also had great importance as the source of a vital wine trade to Britain and northern Europe in general. In the struggle that ensued, Philip was determined to challenge Edward and the English at sea. He, therefore, not only encouraged privateering, which had long been endemic in Norman and Breton ports; he also decided to construct a galley fleet at a new arsenal that he built at Rouen using Provençal and Genoese shipwrights, whom he imported from the Mediterranean. He also employed Genoese mariners as admirals of his new fleet and launched a diplomatic offensive which had as its objective the enlistment on the French side of other Atlantic maritime powers such as Norway and Castile.

Edward responded to this challenge, which endangered his interests in Flanders and Aquitaine, with a naval building program of his own. This program included plans to launch some twenty galleys of a design not yet clear to us, beginning in 1294—not all of which

Town seal of Elbing, 1242, depicting a cog, the popular Hanseatic merchant ship. The stern-post rudder is clearly shown, as is the single mast with clinker construction. Courtesy of the Staatsarchiv, Hamburg.

The seal of Stralsund, 1329. Ships illustrated on seals tend to be rounded to conform to the circular shape of the seal. This one, however, is less stylized than most and shows the sail extended and the ship in motion. Courtesy of the Staatsarchiv, Hamburg.

Second seal of Winchelsea, England, ca 1274. The vessel has a furled sail with seamen at work. The ship is double-ended with a side rudder. Castles have been added fore and aft. National Maritime Museum, Greenwich, England.

Town seal of Elbing, 1350. The ship contrasts sharply with the one depicted on the seal of 1242. It is more rounded and perhaps larger, castles are added, and the mast is sturdier.

Eustace the Monk is decapitated in this scene, a royal triumph over
rebellion and piracy in thirteenth-century England. Various objects
are being fired or thrown by those in the vessel at left after using an
anchor for grappling. As in most battles at sea in this era, losers
were killed or drowned. From the chronicle of Matthew Paris. By
permission of the Masters and Fellows of Corpus Christi College,
Cambridge.

were completed. At the height of the crisis, in 1297, he also raised a
fleet of 305 impressed ships, including about 5,800 sailors, which he
used to carry some 9,000 troops across the narrow seas, a considerable
force indeed. He also reorganized the entire English naval establishment, ashore and on the sea, and, in 1303, instituted for the first time
the formal office of admiral. Though as early as 1230 Henry III had
shown that he could organize a fleet of 288 vessels composed of royal
galleys, Cinque Ports contingents, and impressed merchantmen to
transport his troops to the continent, it was in Edward's time that an
even more effective and permanent English fleet was firmly organized and adequately financed. This fleet made it possible for Edward
to complete the conquest of Wales and Scotland and be well on his
way to conquering Ireland, despite Philip the Fair's efforts to compete
with him on the sea.

Under Edward II, naval forces consisting of royal galleys, Cinque
Ports vessels, and, on occasion, *prizes* of merchant ships continued to
operate, despite the loss of Scotland, weaknesses in Ireland, and the
constant opposition of Edward's barons. Three admirals continued to
be chosen to command separate squadrons in the North Sea, the
Channel, and western England, respectively, and so did a number of
able clerks of the King's Ships, who provided naval and financial administrative continuity.

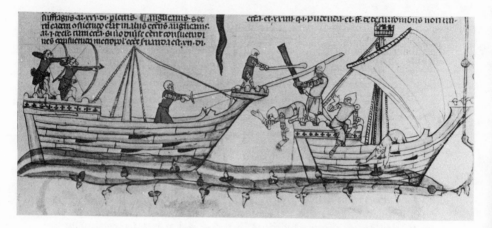

Naval battle from a psalter, ca 1330, showing two cogs. Note the incorporation of the aftercastles into the design of the hull. Upward protruding knees on the gunnels may serve as snatches for the anchors. The archers provide an important advantage. By permission of the British Library. MS. Roy. 10 E. IV, f. 19.

It was, however, only in the 1330s that, during the reign of Edward III, when formal hostilities broke out with France, and Norman, Castilian, and other privateers began to prey on English shipping in the Channel, we again see English naval operations function effectively. By 1340 this organized effort allowed Edward to gather together a fleet of about 300 ships with which he destroyed an opposing Franco-Genoese and Castilian flotilla in the harbor of Sluys. Between 1341 and 1343 he gathered a fleet of some 224 ships for a series of indecisive campaigns in Brittany. And finally, in 1347, he raised an armada of some 738 ships and 15,000 seamen to transport 2,000 soldiers to besiege Calais. Though this naval force represented the high point of Edward's activities at sea, somewhat smaller forces won a great victory over the Castilians off Winchelsea in 1350 in an engagement called *Les Espagnols sur Mer*, and the Black Prince in 1356 was able to assemble a fleet of over 100 ships to carry his forces to France for that campaign in which he won the decisive battle of Poitiers over his French opponents. The strategy and tactics in the sea battles of this era are revealed in the following accounts of the engagements of 1340 and 1350.

In the years of our Lord 1340 . . . the lord king [Edward III] . . . heard that the tyrant of the French had sent a great fleet of Spanish ships and almost all the shipping of the French kingdom to bar his crossing, he called together his ships of the Cinque Ports and elsewhere, so that he had 260 ships, both great and small. . . . He saw the French fleet in the haven of the Zwyn, ready for the fray, and as if ordered in the line of battle; and then, anchoring in the sea, he deliberated the whole day what it would be best to do. On the feast of St. John [24 June], very early in the morning, the French fleet, dividing into three ranks, moved forward a mile toward the royal fleet. When he saw this, the King of England said that he would not wait longer and he and his men ran to arms and were soon ready. After nine o'clock when he had the wind and the sun at his back and the flow of the tide with him, with his ships divided into three columns, he gave his enemies the challenge they wished for. . . . An iron shower of quarrels from crossbows and arrows from long bows brought death to thousands of people; . . . stones hurled from the turrets of masts dashed out the brains of many; to sum up, there was joined without any doubt a great and terrible naval battle. The greatness of the Spanish ships foiled many a stroke of the English; but at last the French ships were overcome, and the first contingent of vessels emptied of men, and the English seized the craft. The French ships were chained together, so that they could not be torn from one another; so a few English guarded one group of the captured ships; the others charged the second contingent. . . . This contingent was, however, more easily emptied than the first, because the French, deserting their ships, for the most part leapt overboard without resisting. . . . During the night thirty ships of the third squadron fled; . . . . When the king realized that 30 ships had fled, he sent 40 well-armed ships to follow them. . . .

The number of warships captured there amounted to 200, and the number of barges taken was thirty. [From Geoffrey le Baker, *Chronicon*, ed. E.M. Thompson (Oxford, 1889), 68–69. In *English Historical Documents, IV* 1327–1485, ed. A.R. Myers (London, 1969), 68–69.]

In the year 1350 while the Spanish were in Flanders for trading purposes, they were told that the English were intending to waylay them on their voyage back home. . . . [They] equipped their ships, lying at Sluys, with all kinds of weapons and powerful artillery, and engaged all the mercenaries, archers and crossbowmen who were willing to serve them for pay. . . . They went on with their purchases of goods . . . [and] waited for each other, so as to sail in one fleet. . . .

The Spanish were coming so fast that, had they wished, they

could have sailed clean through without engaging. They were in big ships, well trimmed, with the wind astern. . . . Instead they prepared to give battle in earnest with their full strength. . . .

When King Edward [III] saw how things were shaping, he called to the helmsman . . . "Steer at that ship straight ahead of us. I want to have a joust at it." . . . . The King's ship was stoutly built and timbered, otherwise it would have been split in two, for it and the Spanish ship, which was tall and heavy, collided with a crash like thunder and as they rebounded, the castle of the King's ship caught the castle of the Spaniard with such force that the mast on which it was fixed broke and it was flung into the sea. The men in it were killed or drowned. The King's ship was so shattered . . . water began to pour in. . . .

Then the king looking at the ship with which he had jousted . . . said, "Grapple my ship to that one. I want to have it." "Let that one go," his knights answered, "You'll get a better one." So that ship went on and another big one came up. The knights flung out hooks and chains and fastened their own ship to it. A fierce battle began between them, the English archers shooting and the Spanish defending themselves lustily. . . . The advantage was by no means with them for, the Spanish ships being bigger and higher than theirs, they were able to shoot down at them and hurl the great iron bars which did considerable damage. The knights in the King of England's ship seeing that it was making so much water it was in danger of foundering, made desperate efforts to capture the ship to which they were grappled. . . . The Spaniard was taken, and all the men on board it thrown into the sea. Only then was the King told of the danger they were in of sinking and urged to move into the ship they had just captured. This he did. . . . But finally the day was with the English. The Spaniards lost fourteen ships, while the rest sailed on and escaped. [Froissart, *Chronicle*, trans. G. Brereton (Harmondsworth, 1968), pp. 113–19.]

Still another way of examining English naval power during this period is to find out from governmental records how many ships and of what sort were built by the Crown. Records suggest that Edward III's government built about fifty vessels of "King's Ships" between 1340 and 1360, a large number of which seem to have been *cogs* rather than galleys, and, after the war had been resumed in 1369, some forty more were built, until the destruction of most of the English fleet by the Castilians off La Rochelle in 1372. The story ends with the sale of many of the remaining ships, following the death of Edward III in 1377, in order to pay the king's debts. The crippled royal fleet was,

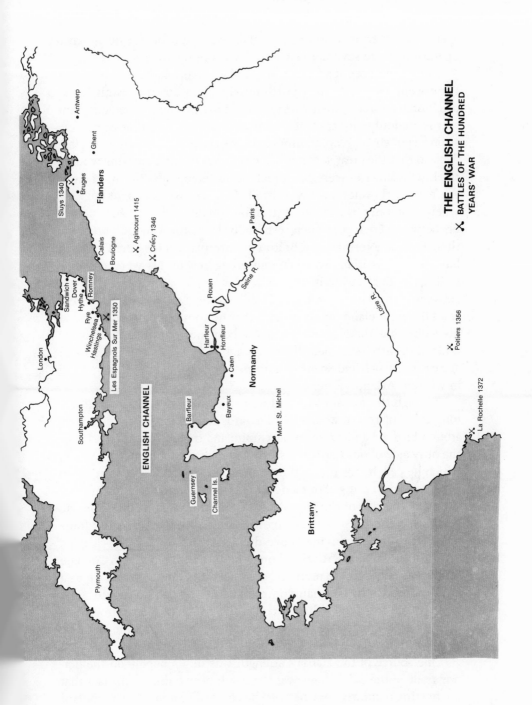

THE ENGLISH CHANNEL

× BATTLES OF THE HUNDRED YEARS' WAR

Antwerp

Ghent

Sluys 1340 ×
Bruges
Flanders

× Agincourt 1415

× Crécy 1346

Calais
Boulogne

Paris

Seine R.

Rouen
Harfleur
Honfleur
Caen
Normandy

Bayeux

Mont St. Michel

Barfleur

Sandwich
Dover
Hythe
Romney
Rye
Winchelsea
Hastings
× Les Espagnols Sur Mer 1350

London

ENGLISH CHANNEL

Southampton

Guernsey
Channel Is.

Brittany

Loire R.

× Poitiers 1356

× La Rochelle 1372

Plymouth

then, clearly treated as the personal possession of the king; naval operations were severely restricted as a consequence.

How effective such fleets were in practice is another matter. That they kept the sea lanes sufficiently open so that English expeditionary forces down to 1372 could always reach the continent seems undoubtedly true. It seems also to be a fact that they were strong enough to keep communications open to Gascony and Flanders, so that the great seasonal wine convoys or ships carrying wool to the Low Countries were never really interfered with. But throughout these years, they never really controlled the narrow seas about England, where not only was there a running privateering struggle carried on between English seamen, especially from the Cinque Ports, and their French, Norman and Breton counterparts across the Channel, but where Castilian, Scottish, and other freebooters were active as well. Even English mariners fought each other at times, as the feud between Yarmouth and Cinque Ports' mariners makes very clear. Edward III might claim on his coinage that he controlled the seas around his realm, but the facts do not really bear him out. Indeed, after his death, England found herself increasingly helpless as she faced more aggressive French and Spanish maritime opponents in the Channel and in western Atlantic waters.

Though the major naval and maritime story during the century-long reign of the three English Edwards from 1272 to 1377 centers around England and her overseas empire and trading interests, it is not the only side of our maritime story. Much was happening elsewhere, which helped, by the end of this period, to erode England's position on the seas and to bring about a new era later on. One cause of this erosion was the rise of the Hanseatic League of maritime cities on the North Sea and the Baltic during the late thirteenth and early fourteenth century, to which we have already briefly alluded. This league, centering in Lübeck with Hamburg, Bremen, and sometimes Cologne serving as subordinate partners, organized the commerce of up to a hundred northern German commercial centers to dominate most trade to and from the Baltic. It controlled much of the commerce in the North Sea, reaching the Netherlands, England, and the Atlantic coast of Norway as well.

One source of the Hansa's strength was its monopoly on the herring trade of the Baltic. This was the result of two things: the fact that the herring regularly spawned off the coast of Scania, and the control

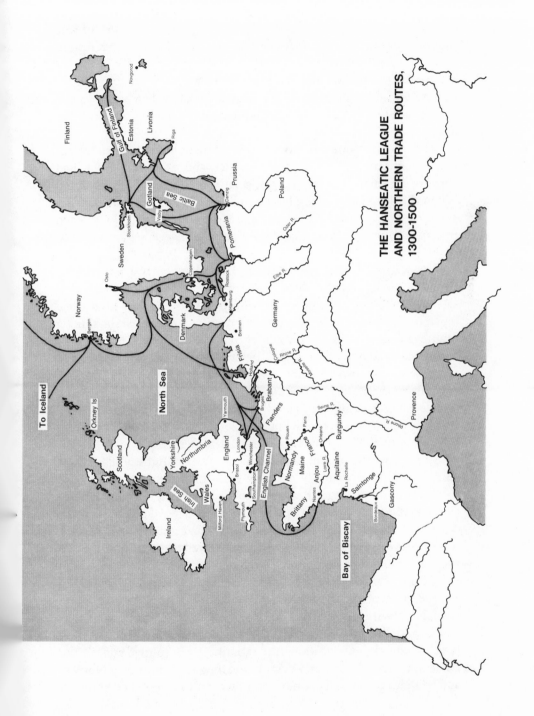

THE HANSEATIC LEAGUE
AND NORTHERN TRADE ROUTES,
1300-1500

Finland

Gulf of Finland

Estonia

Livonia

Novgorod

Riga

Prussia

Poland

Gotland

Baltic Sea

Danzig

Pomerania

Visby

Stockholm

Sweden

Oder R.

Oslo

Copenhagen

Rostock

Norway

Denmark

Hamburg

Bremen

Germany

Elbe R.

Bergen

Frisia

Holland

Coblenz

Rhine R.

Moselle R.

Brabant

To Iceland

North Sea

Orkney Is

Bruges

Flanders

Scotland

Yorkshire

Northumbria

Yarmouth

Rouen

Seine R.

Paris

Burgundy

Wales

England

London

Bristol

Normandy

Orleans

Irish Sea

Milford Haven

Winchester

Maine

France

Anjou

Loire R.

Aquitaine

Provence

Ireland

Plymouth

Southampton

English Channel

Brittany

Nantes

Saintonge

Rhone R.

La Rochelle

Bay of Biscay

Bordeaux

Gascony

by Lübeck and her allies during the late thirteenth century of salt supplies necessary to preserve the herring catch. Thus they were able to exclude English and other North Sea merchants not only from the herring fisheries, but also from all trade with the eastern Baltic. Lübeck, joined by its urban North Sea neighbors, had created a league of cities stretching along Baltic coasts to Danzig and Riga and into the North Sea.

By 1300, this confederation of trading towns had expanded to control Stockholm and the trade of Sweden and, soon thereafter, had come to dominate Norway and, especially, its Atlantic port of Bergen. When the Danes objected, a large Hansa fleet broke their naval power and forced them to accept the treaty of Stralsund of 1370, which ceded to Hansa control Denmark and the Kattegat-Skaggerack entrance to the Baltic.

Nor were these German Hanseatic merchants inactive further to the west. By the early fourteenth century, they had established themselves as the principal suppliers of cheap grain to the Low Countries, replacing England there, and also in Scandinavia, and establishing a privileged *comptor* or trading center in Bruges. Since the English had their eyes fixed upon France and the Bordeaux wine trade, the Hansa was able to establish a similar privileged trading position in England, not only in their *Steelyard* of London, but also in centers of the wool trade such as Boston on England's east coast. In the process they became the chief exporters of English cloth, as well as of that of the Netherlands, to Scandinavia and the Baltic countries.

Soon thereafter, searching for bulk cargoes to fill the holds of their ships, which were already carrying grain, fish, timber, metals and naval stores to the west, they began to load large cargoes of Bourgneuf salt in Britanny and then sail on as far as Lisbon for additional cargoes of wine and salt for the north. By 1350, they had come to operate with little opposition a trading empire which linked the furs of Novgorod, the timber and naval stores of Livonia and Scandinavia, the grain of Poland and Pomerania, the iron of Sweden, the herring of Scania, and the cod of Bergen with the cloth of England and the Netherlands and the salt and wine of Atlantic France and Portugal. Where English merchants and ships had once been supreme, the Hansa now sent regular, large, seasonal convoys along the Atlantic trade routes, and, in the process, managed to utterly destroy the merchant marine of Norway and to reduce that of Denmark and Sweden to impotence and sub-

Arrival of the Earl of Salisbury at Conway Castle, northern Wales. This illustration from the early fifteenth century pays little attention to scale but clearly portrays clinker-built vessels with fore- and aftercastles and a low waist amidships. The ties hanging from the sails are probably reef-points for reducing sail. By permission of the British Library, Harley MS. 1319, f. 14b.

servience. England still maintained a wool staple at Calais after 1350, but the trade this wool had helped to foster to the east, and to the distant Baltic in particular, like much else, was in Hanseatic hands.

The growth of Iberian sea power during the thirteenth century was even more decisive in the long run. We have already commented on this growth down to 1272. Iberian sea power resulted in part from a steady increase throughout the century of trade in iron from the Basque ports of northern Spain, and, especially after 1250, from exports of wine and tropical fruits and fish from Seville, Andalusia and Galicia. Wine and salt exports from Portugal also contributed to the maritime development of the peninsula, especially after King Dinis began to encourage shipping and trading in his great port of Lisbon.

Ship from an illustrated manuscript of 1450-75. The ana-
chronism of the tacked-on fore- and aftercastles must be
balanced against the range of activities depicted as this
vessel is serviced for further duty at sea. Note the early
display of masts rising from the castles. By permission
of the Bodleian Library, MS. Douce 353, f. 31.

Equally important, the Atlantic ports of Iberia, especially Seville
and Lisbon, became the beneficiaries of a trade which originated in
the Mediterranean and which was carried on in specially constructed
Atlantic galleys, which journeyed through the Strait of Gibraltar to
England and the Netherlands. The Genoese began this regular galley
service in the 1270s and were followed soon thereafter by the Venetians and later by Majorcan and Catalan ships from the Aragonese

Empire. The Italians, in particular, carried alum, needed in the manufacture of fine cloth, along with spices, and silks, in return for fine English and Belgian woolen cloth and some specie. They not only settled in large numbers in Iberian Atlantic ports, but also, as noted, served as admirals in the new Castilian and Portuguese navies, as well as, on occasion, those of France and England. Since there were already a number of Italian bankers and tax officials in key positions in the financial and governmental world of Seville, Lisbon, London, Bruges, and Paris, their ships and cargoes moved almost everywhere and received important trading privileges. Overall, of course, their activities most benefited the Iberian maritime interests with which they were closely associated.

Finally, this century saw the development of a great Castilian sheep industry, whose prized merino wool produced by the royal-backed *Mesta* could, by the late fourteenth century, compete successfully in the Netherlands and elsewhere with the finest English varieties, giving Castilian traders, already prosperous from their trade in iron, copper, fruits, wine, and fish to the north, another valuable export commodity. No wonder we find by the fourteenth century large colonies of Iberian merchants in English and Netherland ports and Iberian ships operating in large numbers in the English Channel.

The economic and maritime importance of the Iberian Peninsula helps us to understand why Philip the Fair and his successors made every effort to enlist Castilians in their war at sea against the English in the days of both Edward I and Edward III and why Castilian ships were among those encountered at Sluys in 1340 and a decade later in the battle of *Les Espagnols sur Mer* in the Channel, which we have described in detail above. It also explains why the English were willing to intervene in Castile to support Pedro the Cruel, one of two claimants to the throne. Unfortunately for them, though they won a great battle at Nájera in 1367 over Pedro's Castilian opponents and their French allies, Pedro was assassinated soon thereafter and the English failed in their objectives.

The result, as we know, was the loss of the Castilian fleet as an ally, and the destruction of English sea power off La Rochelle in 1372, which is described in the following excerpt from Froissart.

King Charles of France [in 1372] by some means became perfectly acquainted with the greater part of the King of England's

plans, and secretly raised a large naval armament for the purposes
of a war with him; that is to say, it was done at his request, for the
navy belonged to King Henry of Castille. . . . This fleet consisted
of forty large vessels and thirteen barks, well provided with towers and ramparts, and was placed under the command of four val-
iant men. . . . When the Earl of Pembroke and his fleet expected to
enter the port of La Rochelle, they found that the Spaniards had
blocked up the entrance by lying before its mouth. . . . The English . . . made themselves ready for immediate combat. The engagement was very severe . . . for the Spaniards who were in large
ships had with them great bars of iron and huge stones, which
they launched from their own vessels in order to sink those of the
English. . . . The battle lasted until night, when each party separated and cast anchor. . . .

The next day, at high tide, the Spaniards weighed anchor, and
with a great noise of trumpets and drums formed a line of battle,
and endeavored to enclose the English, who, observing the ma-
noeuvre, drew up their ships accordingly, placing their archers in
front. As soon as they came to close quarters the Spaniards threw
out grappling hooks, which lashed the vessels together, so that
they could not separate. The contest continued with great fury
until nearly nine o'clock, when the Earl of Pembroke's ship was
boarded, himself made prisoner, and all with him either taken or
slain. At some distance the Poitevins under command of Sir
Guiscard d'Angle continued to fight; but the Spaniards were too
many for them. . . . On the afternoon of the day the Spaniards set
their sails and departed, much rejoiced at their victory. [Froissart,
Chronicles, trans. T. Johnes (New York, 1901), pp. 139–40.]

Though John of Gaunt tried in vain to recapture Castile for his daughter and England in the 1380s, he had to content himself with a less
vital Portuguese alliance.

The sea power of the Hansa crept out of the Baltic to take over
from England in the North Sea, the Channel, and beyond while she
was busy fighting in France, and that of Iberia, and especially of Castile,
did the same from the Atlantic, initiating by 1377 a new maritime age
which we will be examining in the next chapter.

The period between 1066 and 1377 is marked by important
changes in the ships used in warfare and in trade in northern Europe—
much more important changes, as a matter of fact, than were made in
ships of the Mediterranean. These changes were due to the steady
increase in the shipping of bulk cargoes in the northern seas. Though
we have already noted that by the late tenth century some bulk car-

goes already had begun to be transported by sea in northern Europe, such trade increased immensely in the twelfth and thirteenth centuries. For instance, England's maritime preponderance during these two centuries was based upon three primary raw materials, which formed the major cargoes of her merchant vessels: wheat, sent to Scandinavia and Gascony; wool, shipped in large wool sacks across the North Sea to Belgium; and wine, coming first from Saintogne and later from Gascony. In return, the English imported large amounts of dried cod from Norway and salted herring from the Baltic states, as well as some iron from Basque and Cantabrian ports.

By the fourteenth century, certain changes in bulk cargoes had taken place. Baltic grain replaced English, except in trade with Gascony, and both the Netherlands and England, having exhausted most of their best timber, imported it from Scandinavia and Livonia. New use was also made of the cheap and abundant salt of Bourgneuf Bay and Portugal, and Bordeaux and Rhenish wine now had to compete with vintages from Andalusia and Portugal. Just as copper and iron from Sweden often replaced Iberian metals in northern markets, we now find cod from Iceland competing with that from Bergen in the British Isles. Even more so than in the Mediterranean, where salt, grain, timber, metals, and cotton formed the backbone of seaborne trades, the maritime commerce of the north had become essentially a bulk affair.

Sometimes this traffic was huge in volume. For instance, English records show that in the first decades of the fourteenth century some one thousand ships averaging about 250 tons each annually carried about 72,700 large casks of wine to northern European ports, mainly in the British Isles. This wine fleet, incidentally, was approximately as large as all the ships of the Venetians, or those of the Hanseatic League, put together. Toward the end of this same century, the Hansa could count on an annual catch of some 100,000 casks of herring, which they distributed to ports around the northern seas in some five hundred large- and medium-sized cogs. And between 1330 and 1350 England's annual export of wool amounted to between 30,000 and 35,000 woolsacks a year, which was a slight decrease from the 40,000 to 45,000 that was the average in the early years of the century. Custom receipts levied by Edward I brought in six to seven times more annual revenue than those imposed by John between 1202 and 1204, and Edward III, as noted, could impress some 700 merchant ships for an overseas expedition. Though the Black Death of 1348–50 and its recurrence in the 1360s may have halved the population of this part of Europe, which in turn reduced the wine trade of Gascony late in the century to one-third of its former volume, it is surprising how much bulk cargo still traveled by sea in the north right down to 1377.

The prevalence of bulk cargoes does not mean that other more lucrative cargoes were not carried on the merchant vessels of the time. The large, oared galleys used by Genoa, Venice, and the Catalans on their Atlantic runs to the north—ships which carried valuable alum and Mediterranean spices and luxury goods north in exchange for fine English and Belgian woolens and metalware—are the proof of this. And after 1350 England increasingly exported woolen cloth instead of raw wool to overseas customers. But maritime traffic was composed mostly of bulk goods moving from the areas of Europe which produced raw materials to its growing urban centers.

The ships that carried these cargoes in the north reflected this state of affairs. In Scandinavia and along eastern English shores, the small, single-masted, clinker-built *knarrs* and *keels* of the tenth century became larger in size or were replaced by *busses*, which had six or seven times the cargo capacity of their earlier prototypes. Even more important was the development of the *cog*, which not only increased in size to become a single-masted, clinker-built vessel of 250 tons, but also added a keel and a steering rudder, in place of oars, to make it more seaworthy in the open ocean. The *cog* was joined on long voyages from the North Sea into the Baltic by way of the Kattegat-Skaggerack route by larger versions of the earlier *hulk*, now also clinker-built and using a stern rudder. *Cogs* were also used extensively in trade passing through the English Channel and formed much of the wine fleet which annually sailed north from Bordeaux, though in these Atlantic waters large barges, descended from the *barcas* of an earlier age, were also used.

Smaller craft were also used in the coastal trades and in traffic that flowed about the narrow seas of the north, especially in the Baltic. Such craft may even have carried a large part of the cargoes which traveled on the seaways, just as *lengs* and *nefs* did in the western Mediterranean. We know, for example, that *knarrs* continued to sail to Iceland and Greenland throughout these years and that small fishing vessels were used everywhere in the North Sea and in the Channel

The Bremen cog of ca 1350–1400 was found in the River Weser in 1962. Rated at 130 tons, the ship is 77' (23.5 m.) long and 23' (7 m.) amidship. Courtesy of the Deutsches Schiffahrtsmuseum, Bremerhaven.

and even on longer runs from Galicia, Brittany, or western England to Icelandic fishing grounds. The ubiquitous *cog*, along with the *hulk* in the Baltic, the barge in the Atlantic, and the *buss* in Norwegian waters, however, were the trading ships par excellence during these centuries.

As for warships, much the same thing is true. The *cog*, with permanent or temporary fore and aft castles added to it and a crow's nest near the top of the mast, had become the most important warship of the late thirteenth and fourteenth centuries, though not the only one in use. We know that as late as 1263 huge *drekkars* were built in Scandinavia and that perhaps some of the galleys built by Edward I, II, and III followed the same design. We also have pointed out a bit earlier that the Genoese, in 1302, built Mediterranean-type galleys for the French king in his arsenal at Rouen and that other galleys of an Atlantic type were used in the Castilian and Portuguese fleets of the fourteenth century and perhaps in English ones as well. There were also a number of small warships such as those small, swift sailing ships used by seamen of the Cinque Ports or the oared *balingers* and other

The Bremen cog viewed from the stern during reconstruction. The
aftercastle was attached after construction of the hull and was not
incorporated in the overall design. Courtesy of Detlev Ellmers,
Deutsches Schiffahrtsmuseum, Bremerhaven.

small craft employed by both sides in the Channel, whose actual design is uncertain. Ship design in the north had begun to catch up with
that in the Mediterranean during this period.

When we turn to advances in navigation, however, we find that at
the close of the fourteenth century we have little evidence that the
superior compass of the Mediterranean had spread widely in Atlantic
and northern waters even though it was derived from a northern prototype. Instead of navigating with portolan charts, northern seamen
still preferred to use sailing directions or rutters, or even lead and line,
to navigate in their narrow seas.

On the other hand, there is considerable evidence of an improve-
ment in the technical and tactical way naval power was deployed.
Though Sluys represented a typical slugging match in harbor, like
Damme a century earlier, by the time of *Les Espagnols sur Mer* and *La
Rochelle*, as we have made clear, we find naval battles were beginning

View of the Bremen cog from the bow on the port side showing the clinker construction and the framing timbers to which the planking is attached. Courtesy of the Deutsches Schiffahrtsmuseum, Bremerhaven.

to be fought at sea, as was the case previously in the Mediterranean. And in northern naval encounters, crossbowmen were now placed in the rigging, and catapults and other pelteries were used as well. Although we find no evidence of the kind of sophisticated amphibious operations similar to those used by Crusading fleets in the south or of artillery on ships, which Italians had begun to show could be employed successfully, the gap which had existed in technical and tactical naval practices between north and south had all but ended by 1377.

Such improvement was less true of financial operations which affected maritime operations, in part because of the special financial role played by England during these centuries. England, as we have noted, occupied a central position in the north as regards maritime matters from 1066 until the death of Edward III. During these years she was unusual in maintaining a silver coinage on a national scale

Carved bench-end, ca 1415, from the Church of St. Nicholas (the patron saint of mariners) in Kings Lynn. The lateen mizzen is clearly shown. Victoria and Albert Museum, London.

A "round ship" built in the clinker style in a fifteenth-century Flemish artist's rendition of Jason's quest for the Golden Fleece. The crewman is working from clearly illustrated ratlines. By permission of the British Library. MS. Harley 4425, f. 86.

which remained relatively unchanged in value except under Edward III from 1335 to 1352. As a result, this coinage or *sterling*, as it was known, became the basis for most commercial transactions in northern waters. It was also very abundant. For instance, when Richard the Lion-Hearted needed to be ransomed from captivity, his mother, Eleanor of Aquitaine, was able to raise thousands of pounds of silver in a very short period to pay off his Hohenstaufen enemies on the continent and get him released. Again, in the mid-thirteenth century, when the English king, Henry III, decided to let his brother, Richard of Cornwall, call in the old coins and issue new ones, we know that, over fourteen years, a million pounds of silver was reminted. About 1300, when Edward I decided to do the same thing, he was able to remint one million pounds of silver coins again—this time over a period of only five years. Such masses of excellent silver coin in circulation made it less necessary for merchants in England or trading with England to develop the same kind of credit instruments or money of account found in Venice, Genoa, or Florence during these years. It made the north, in a sense, financially backward in its development of commercial credit and explains also why attempts to issue gold coins in England and France during the period from the mid-thirteenth century to 1377 were not very successful.

The tremendous expenses incurred by both Edward I and Edward III in carrying on their wars, and especially their naval operations, forced these monarchs to make use of skilled Italian financiers and business methods to anticipate their revenues, especially during the first decades of the Hundred Years War. When Edward III found he could not meet the heavy interest payments on the money Italian bankers had advanced him, he not only defaulted, and thus helped to ruin the Bardi and Peruzzi banking empires, but also was able to switch quite smoothly to native English and German merchants, who from then on financed his war expenses and handled his debts.

This sophistication in public finance in Britain was matched by a considerable private financial sophistication in nobles such as Richard of Cornwall and in merchants of the Staple; and, if we can believe *The King's Mirror*, the same thing was true in thirteenth-century Norway among the Cahorsins, who financed most of Bordeaux's wine trade to the north, and in the Baltic and North sea region among those great financiers and merchants of the Hansa, who handled the business side of the league's trading empire, and among merchant bankers of Bruges and Ghent, such as the Arnolfini. By the late fourteenth century, northern Europe had not yet developed the same kind of banking facilities found in Italy, Catalonia, or Provence. Her merchants had not yet learned to share capital risk through the kind of marine insurance common in Italy. We have no evidence that they had as yet moved beyond partnerships into what we can regard as stock companies or were yet aware of the advantages of double-entry bookkeeping. But they were not far behind southern Europe in the way that they were financing trade and war at sea, and they were moving fast to close the gap.

CHAPTER VII

The Rise of Iberian Sea Power and a New Atlantic Destiny, 1377–1498

THE YEARS FROM 1377 TO 1498 represent a period quite different from that examined in our last chapter. During this century and a quarter, Iberian sea power, already growing in importance, finally came of age, not only in both northern and southern Europe, but also as the leader in the age of overseas expansion. If there was another area of northern Europe which shared in some measure in this maritime leadership though, it was the Netherlands, where the Valois dukes of Burgundy furnished effective government until they became part of a Hapsburg patrimony soon to be linked with the Spain of Ferdinand and Isabella.

As a result, neither England nor the Hansa could any longer furnish the naval and maritime leadership they had exercised down to 1377 in northern waters. Their decline in importance was shared even more dramatically by Scandinavia and France, even though the latter had the advantage of the effective government of her late fifteenth-century kings, Charles VIII and Louis XI.

Let us begin by reviewing some facts about the rise of Iberian sea power mentioned in our previous chapter. This sea power began to assume some importance when, after the Moors were driven out of most of the Iberian Peninsula, the Aragonese, Castilians, and Portuguese began to develop some special naval and maritime expertise, often with Italian help, which they exercised on both sides of the Strait of Gibraltar. Their shipping and commercial activities extended along Atlantic shores as far as the North Sea, where Castilian iron, wine, and wool found ready markets in English, northern French, and especially Belgian ports. Portuguese wine and salt, which competed with that of Gascony and Brittany, did equally well in these same parts of Europe and beyond as far as the Baltic. At the same time, Castilian naval forces, led by Genoese admirals, played a decisive role in helping to destroy English naval strength in the narrow seas surrounding the British Isles.

While this activity was going on in the North Atlantic, Iberian sea power was also beginning to move into southern Atlantic waters, an area which had already been partially explored by Islamic mariners from Spain and Morocco. This area, which a recent distinguished scholar of maritime history has referred to as "the Atlantic Mediterranean," comprises the west coast of Africa and the offshore islands—the Cape Verde, the Canaries, Madeira, and the Azores—that lie to the west. Soon after 1250, Portuguese and Castilian seamen, along with a number of Italians who served Iberian monarchs, as well as some Catalans and Majorcans, rediscovered these islands and proceeded down African shores as far as the Gold Coast. It seems also clear that the famous Portuguese *volta,* by which ships sailed north from the west coast of Africa by going far out into the Atlantic and then letting the westerlies carry them back to the Iberian Peninsula, dates from the early fourteenth rather than from the fifteenth century. And it is equally interesting that the famous Catalan map of 1375, drawn in Majorca, shows not only most of these offshore islands and the west coast of Africa, but also depicts off Guinea shores a Catalan ship which bears the date 1346.

Despite all this nautical knowledge and exploration, however, prior to 1400 no permanent settlements were established in either the islands or along the African coast and the knowledge of them seems to have declined for some decades. Probably this decline was one of the effects of the Black Death, which decimated the maritime population in Iberian ports, and because the Portuguese and Castilians were engaged in constant strife and civil war during the last years of the fourteenth century, inhibiting maritime activities in south Atlantic

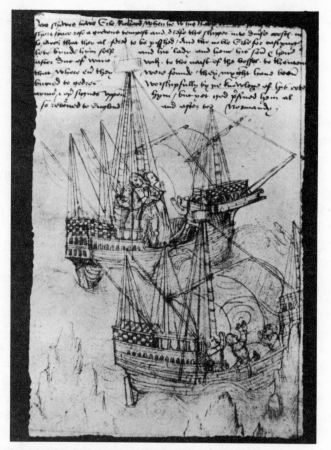

A storm in the English Channel from a scene in the life
of Richard Beauchamp, Earl of Warwick, 1485–90. The
multimasted ships have mizzens with lateen sails. By
permission of the British Library. MS. Julius E. IV, f. 25.

waters. As for the Aragonese, during these same years they suffered a
severe maritime decline, which ended their trade with northern
Europe by sea and adversely affected Barcelona's and Majorca's prosperity in general.

Whatever the reasons for this lull, it ended in the second decade of
the fifteenth century, when the Iberian advance into Atlantic waters
was resumed. This time it was the Portuguese who took the initiative
under the leadership of a member of their royal house whom we know
as Prince Henry the Navigator. Henry and his brother organized a

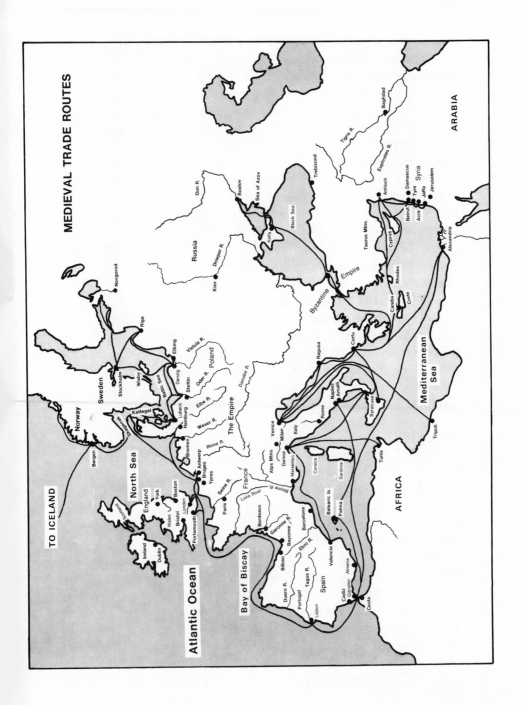

MEDIEVAL TRADE ROUTES

TO ICELAND

Atlantic Ocean

North Sea

Bay of Biscay

Mediterranean Sea

AFRICA

ARABIA

Norway
Bergen

Sweden
Stockholm

Kattegat
Skagerrak

Baltic Sea

Wisby

Riga

Novgorod

Russia

Dnieper R.

Kiev

Don R.

Rostov

Sea of Azov

Kaffa

Black Sea

Trebizond

Tigris R.

Baghdad

Euphrates R.

Antioch
Damascus
Syria
Tyre
Beirut
Acre
Jaffa
Jerusalem

Alexandria

Taurus Mtns.

Cyprus

Rhodes

Candia
Crete

Corfu

Byzantine Empire

Ragusa

Tripoli

Tunis

Sardinia

Corsica

Balearic Is.
Palma

Almeria
Ceuta
Gibraltar
Cadiz

Lisbon

Valencia

Ebro R.

Barcelona

Bayonne
Bordeaux
Garonne R.

Spain

Portugal
Tagus R.

Duero R.

Bilbao

Loire River

Seine R.

Paris

France

Rhone R.

Alps Mtns.

Marseilles

Genoa

Milan

Venice

Italy

Rome

Naples
Amalfi

Syracuse

Rhine R.

The Empire

Weser R.

Elbe R.

Danube R.

Odra R.
Poland

Vistula R.

Elbing
Danzig

Stettin

Hamburg
Bremen
Lubeck

Antwerp
Bruges
Ypres

England
York
Boston
London
Bristol
Wales
Portsmouth

Scotland

Ireland
Dublin

flotilla which, in 1415, captured the port of Ceuta from its Moroccan suzerains and, in doing so, opened up an entrance into the Mediterranean for northern European shipping that Castile and her allies could not deny to them.

Though Henry's motives from this time on seem to have been essentially those of a medieval crusader eager to strike a blow against Islam, not those of a modern expansionist, he followed up this victory with a series of naval expeditions down the coast of Africa as far south as Senegal and the Cape Verde Islands and out into the Atlantic to Madeira and the Azores. Under his aegis the colonization of Madeira began, and his expeditions paid for themselves with gold dust and other commodities that they gathered along the African coast, of which the most valuable were human: blacks brought back to Portugal as slaves and introduced as a labor force into the Algarve and offshore islands.

After Henry's death in 1460, the Portuguese conquered most of the ports of Atlantic Morocco and continued to expand along African coasts, establishing trading posts on offshore islands and exploiting the gold of Ghana and the spices of Nigeria. By 1480 they reached the Congo. A war with Castile between 1476 and 1479 delayed advances for a time and gave the Castilians a clear title to the Canaries. Immediately thereafter, during the reign of Juan II, progress down the coast was resumed, culminating in Bartholomeu Diaz's voyage around the Cape of Good Hope in 1487.

Recognizing what lay ahead, the Portuguese king sent Pero da Covilhão on a secret mission to scout out ports on the east African shore and a decade later organized a final large expedition led by Vasco da Gama, which sailed all the way to south India in 1498 and then returned to Portugal laden with spices. A new route to the East from the Atlantic had been opened up.

Meanwhile, Castile, which had been united with Aragon in 1479 under Ferdinand and Isabella, concerned itself with the conquest of the last Islamic holding in Spain, the kingdom of Granada. Not until 1492 was this conquest completed, and only then did Isabella feel able to give backing to the Genoese mariner, Christopher Columbus, who planned to sail west across the Atlantic and reach the Indies by another route. Columbus, incidentally, had already had his venture turned down by the Portuguese king, whom he had served as captain for more than a decade and whose eye was fixed on the route to India around Africa. The rulers of France and England were equally skeptical of Columbus's plans.

After Columbus returned successfully from the New World in 1493, almost at once Spain and Portugal persuaded Pope Alexander VI to divide the non-European world between them, with all territory discovered a hundred leagues west of the Azores going to Spain, that to the east to Portugal. A year later, in 1494, during Columbus's second voyage to the New World, when he was carrying colonists, the Portuguese negotiated a modification of this Treaty of Tordesillas—a modification that allotted the entire coast of Brazil to Portugal— suggesting that they knew land existed there and were unwilling to let it become Spanish. But only in 1500, after Pedro Cabral's voyage there, did they openly claim it for their empire. At any rate, by 1500 the Spanish and Portuguese had begun a new chapter in European maritime history by moving out to colonize the offshore islands of the south Atlantic, by planting way stations along African shores all the way to India, and by laying claim to Brazil and the West Indies. Iberian sea power had broken the barrier of the Atlantic and moved western Europe toward a new destiny.

Turning north from Iberia along the sea lanes which stretched from the Bay of Biscay to the Baltic, let us consider England, which had emerged as a relatively weak realm after the death of Edward III in 1377. Edward was succeeded by his young grandson, Richard II. Almost immediately, England suffered a series of disasters at home and abroad. In 1381 she had to face the disorders of a serious peasant revolt, and she lost so much of Aquitaine to the French that, when peace was finally made in 1380, her control was restricted to a small area near Bordeaux, which by now could ship only a fifth of the wine exported earlier in the century. In Flanders the pro-English faction was ousted and commercial relations worsened with the growth of French influence.

During this same period, efforts to control the Hansa's near monopoly on trade between England and the Baltic, the Netherlands, and Scandinavia had to be abandoned, and the privileges of this body were renewed and strengthened. And to the north, Scotland asserted its independence from English governance.

Finally, not only was England unable to defend herself in the Channel from French and Spanish naval forces, which burnt ports such as Southampton as the fleet was allowed to decay, but she also lost out in wars waged in Castile to extend English influence there. By 1380, all that she had gained in the Iberian Peninsula was a treaty with Portugal. Castile, like France, the Netherlands, the Hansa, and Scotland, remained either essentially hostile or capable of ignoring English interests. It was a depressed, weak, and disorganized England that saw Richard II overthrown by his cousin Henry IV in 1399—one that Henry II, Edward I, or Edward III would have felt was hardly recognizable, especially from a maritime point of view.

A change took place when, in 1413, young Henry V succeeded his father as king and almost at once launched a new invasion of France. Henry's success in this renewal of the Hundred Years War owed something to his rebuilding of the English fleet, which had been allowed almost to disappear, as well as to the military genius he displayed at the battle of Agincourt in 1415. Henry V's new fleet remained a force for some two decades in keeping the Channel open between England and her conquered French lands. But it was French disunity, an alliance with Burgundy, and the good luck of capturing James I of Scotland on the sea and being able to neutralize Scotland by holding him captive, rather than any real maritime strength, which made England again a factor of importance in the northern seas.

Then, in the first third of the fifteenth century, England displayed a flurry of activity on the sea. Control of the shores of northern France and the Burgundian alliance put an end to piracy and privateering in the English Channel, allowing English ships in some numbers to sail safely south past Portugal, on to Ceuta, and into the Mediterranean as far east as the island of Sicily, which was now in the firm control of the King of Aragon. Other English vessels were welcomed in the ports of Norway and Denmark, which were trying to break the grip of the Hanseatic League on their commerce. Queen Margaret united Norway and Denmark with Sweden and proclaimed their bond in the Union of Kalmar of 1397. Some of these English traders were organized by a group of merchant adventurers, chartered by the Crown in 1407, who somewhat later on carried English cloth into the Baltic all the way to Prussia and Livonia despite the efforts of Lübeck to forbid such commerce in 1426. Still other vessels sailed to Iceland for cod in defiance of Hanseatic prohibitions or competed with Hansa herring in northern markets with herring caught in large numbers in the North Sea.

Few of these maritime initiatives, though, were to last beyond

1435. By then, the Burgundians had made peace with France, deserting their English allies, and had begun to institute the first of a series of trade embargoes against the import of English goods within their domains—especially English cloth. Inspired by Joan of Arc, France rapidly slipped away from English control, until by 1453 Calais alone remained in England's hands. The Hansa again successfully barred English ships from the Baltic and from ports in Norway and Iceland, too, while maintaining its own privileges in Britain. The English fleet was disbanded, and the "king's ships" were sold as Henry VI's government in effect collapsed. The anonymous author of *The Libel of English Polycie*, a pro-naval treatise written in 1437, advised his countrymen to control the seas around Britain and espoused a kind of mercantilism as an answer to her economic and maritime troubles, but little was done to remedy things until after 1485. The following example of the hostilities that England faced is from the text of a treaty negotiated in 1443 between Castile and the German Hansa.

> To the glory of the Blessed Trinity and so that their commerce may grow to mutual advantage, the nations of the German Hansa and Spain . . . have thus reached agreement. . . .
> All merchants, sailors and subjects of the German nations and German Hansa will be free to travel, settle and stay as they will in every region, town and port belonging to his gracious Majesty the King of Castile, and to take with them their goods, possessions, merchandise and retinues. . . .
> Should it so happen that Hanseatic sailors, having left a port and reached the high seas in company with Spanish sailors, encounter enemies of the Spanish such as the English, they will straightway hoist their flags or any other signal to indicate that they are not enemies. They will then withdraw to one side so as not to encumber the Spanish sailors in their fight against their enemies. . . .
> The two sides agree that the merchants of the German nation, whenever they acquire wine or other commodities at the port of La Rochelle, should give preference to loading them in greater quantities on Spanish ships than on ships of any other nation. . . .
> [P. Dollinger, *The German Hansa*, trans. D.S. Ault and S.H. Steinberg (Stanford, 1970), pp. 392–93.]

It was the Tudor king, Henry VII, who at last set England upon a new maritime course which was to bring her future greatness. Until then, however, except for the first few decades of the century, England remained a minor factor in the maritime and naval scheme of things in northern Europe.

The failure of English efforts to maintain a position of maritime and naval preponderance during the years after 1377 was matched by a similar lack of success on the part of the Hanseatic League. This lack, in part, was because there was no effective governing body to coordinate the Hansa's interests, which allowed Cologne in the west and the Wendish towns in the eastern Baltic to pursue policies which were at times hostile to Lübeck, the heart and soul of the league and its most important member. In part, it was due to the growing restiveness of the Scandinavian realms, which chafed under the Hansa's monopoly on their outside trade and which were uniting to undermine the league's dominance in northern waters. It was also because a new and important herring industry had begun in the North Sea, allowing Dutch, English, and Scottish fishermen who were exploiting this resource to compete successfully with the Hansa fishermen who caught herring off Scania in the Baltic. And English, Breton, and Basque fishermen were now catching cod off Iceland, enabling them to compete with the fisheries of the Löfoten Islands near Bergen.

By the first decades of the fifteenth century, the Hansa was so weakened that both English vessels and a new fleet of Netherlander merchantmen could sail into the Baltic and trade directly with Wendish and Livonian towns. Lübeck got the *Hansetag*, the league's assembly, to pass legislation in 1426 barring foreign ships in these waters. But this prohibition proved ineffective as far as the Netherlanders were concerned. Though English ships, especially after 1435, were, on the whole, excluded from this trade, those from the Low Countries were not, and, in increasing numbers throughout the rest of the century, they sailed past Copenhagen carrying cloth and other manufactured wares and finished goods as far east as Riga and Danzig to exchange for grain, timber, naval stores, and metals. And they carried on increasing commerce with Bergen, Oslo, and other Norwegian ports. Though the Hanseatic League maintained its *comtor* at Bruges for the rest of the century, increasingly found itself at a commercial disadvantage in the maritime trade it carried on with the Netherlands.

What was the overall maritime position of the Netherlands during these years when both England and the Hanseatic League were ex-

periencing serious difficulties? They were enjoying a period of increasing commercial and maritime prosperity. It is hard not to view
this rise of Netherlander maritime enterprise as due in no small measure to the policies of Duke Philip the Good of Burgundy (1419–
1467), who, while he was allied with the English and supporting their
advances in northern France, was uniting the Netherlands politically
in a number of ways. During the years down to 1435, the English
alliance allowed his subjects to trade freely in the Channel and in
English ports, and to survive a change in the location of the Flemish
cloth industry from its old centers in Ghent and Bruges to new ones in
Brabant and Holland. Peace with the French king in 1435 increased
trade with northern France, and traffic up the Rhine and Moselle to
the heart of western Europe became even more vital during the next
few decades as well. Increased commerce with the world of the Hansa
in Scandinavia and the Baltic allowed the Netherlanders to import
cheap timber and naval stores, in order to build their ships economically, and cheap grain to feed their urban population.

Trade embargoes periodically directed against English cloth exports hurt the English more than the Low Countries because after
1450 the fine wool needed for the Netherlands' cloth industry could
be imported from Spain rather than from the British Isles. Also, ships
sailing to Iberian ports could bring back wine from Portugal and Gascony, cheap salt from Britanny, and iron from the Basque country.
This cheap salt, in turn, gave the Dutch an important resource for
curing the herring of the North Sea, which they began to ship south to
Iberian ports. A whole network of maritime activities from Lisbon to
Riga and Bergen had come to center in the Low Countries.

When Charles the Rash, the last Burgundian duke to control the
Netherlands, died in 1477 and his daughter, Mary, wed the Emperor
Maximilian, the Netherlands were linked to Austrian possessions in
central Europe, where a mining boom was taking place. The Fuggers
and Welsers, the beneficiaries of this mining boom and closely associated with Maximilian, soon decided to transfer the center of their
business operations to the Low Countries, with headquarters in Antwerp. Here, by 1500, a truly modern, freewheeling, capitalist trading and
banking center had already made its appearance, from which the great
Dutch enterprises of the sixteenth and seventeenth centuries were to
arise.

Were there other important centers of trade in Europe during this period other than an expanding Iberia, a prosperous Netherlands, and the somewhat decayed maritime centers of the Hansa and England? Certainly northern and Atlantic France was one, especially Brittany and Normandy after the English had been expelled about the middle of the fifteenth century. Brittany benefited, in particular, from the salt produced in large amounts near the mouth of the Loire. Its seamen were able to employ a fleet of relatively small vessels to peddle this salt to ports all around the northern seas. The salt also cured the cod which its fishing flotilla brought back in increasing volume from north Atlantic waters, enabling it to compete with British rivals from Bristol and other west country ports.

Norman maritime enterprise also was able to expand after Normandy had been recovered by the French king in 1447. The Normans maintained an active trade in the Channel, partly as a result of their cloth industry, and partly since the Seine served as an entryway for goods moving to and from Paris. Normandy also benefited from the reopening of the royal arsenal of Rouen, where Charles VII and Louis XI again began to build ships for an Atlantic fleet, while Norman mariners in other ports returned to their old practice of privateering in the Channel. Although relatively unimportant from a maritime point of view when compared to Iberia, the Netherlands, or even the British Isles, Brittany and Normandy in these years laid the foundations of later French naval and commercial power in the gray waters of the western Atlantic.

Finally, we need to turn to the maritime standing of Scandinavia and of the north Atlantic in general—a much-discussed and controversial subject. By the late fourteenth century, Scandinavian maritime enterprise in both Norway and Denmark was able to display few signs of its old vitality, thanks to the shackles of the Hansa, which strangled native initiative on the sea. Perhaps the Black Death of mid-century, which halved the port population, also played a role. At any rate, we know that after 1348 the annual ship from Norway to Greenland ceased to make the trip, and traffic between Bergen and Iceland was reduced to a trickle. The advent of the little Ice Age, during which the ice pack enlarged and glaciers advanced south, was also of significance. We know that at about this time the northern Norse settlement in Greenland was abandoned, and a new group of Eskimos arrived in this part of the island from the west.

Archeological evidence, however, has revealed to us that the other, more southerly Greenland settlement continued to maintain an existence of its own, though its inhabitants, based on skeletal evidence, were stunted and malnourished. But clothing found during the excavation of graves reflects styles which did not appear in western Europe until 1450, suggesting that some contacts with Europe continued right down to the time of Columbus—contacts which were perhaps made with English, Basque, or Iberian fishermen, or with whalers who ventured into these northern waters.

Did such contacts extend to the North American mainland, which the Greenlanders had periodically visited since the twelfth century to procure timber and Arctic furs—as a certain amount of archeological evidence from Canada strongly suggests? It seems probable. At any rate, we have some rather interesting evidence from the west of England which shows that Bristol fishermen sailed to the Grand Banks off Newfoundland and Labrador for some ten years before John Cabot's voyage there in 1498, in the service of Henry VII. During this same decade, Basque and Portuguese fishermen probably also exploited these waters in pursuit of the cod beyond Iceland, as the Portuguese name, Labrador, suggests. Such activity would explain why the king of a united Norway and Denmark, in the last years of the fifteenth century, thought it worthwhile to give backing to a joint Danish-Portuguese expedition which sailed beyond Greenland and into Hudson's Bay and so began a more formal exploration of the Atlantic shores of North America. At the same time that the Castilians under Columbus's command and the Portuguese were sailing across the Atlantic to the West Indies and Brazil, and the Portuguese were sailing around the Cape of Good Hope to India, northern European fishermen and seamen were reaching the shores of North America, despite unfavorable climatic conditions, as they pursued the cod and the whale into waters where Irish and Scandinavian seamen had ventured centuries earlier.

The ravages of the Black Death between 1348 and 1350 resulted in a tremendous overall drop in Europe's population, perhaps halving it before it began to increase again. However, most of the trends noted in maritime trade about the northern seas continued— especially the emphasis upon bulk cargoes. Grain, timber, naval stores, metals, fish, and some valuable furs were still the principal exports from Scandinavia and the Baltic, and wine, salt, wool, and

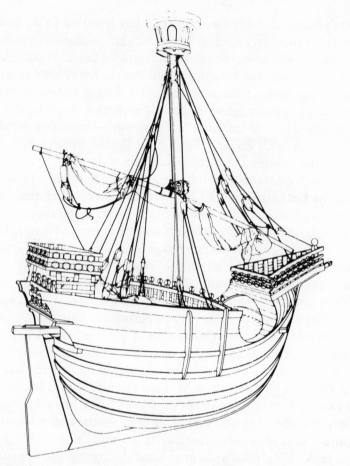

Model of a fifteenth-century Spanish caravel from Mataró, in northern Spain, where it probably served as a votive ship in the Chapel of
St. Simon. The Mataró model is the only existing three-dimensional
ship from this period. The staff of the Maritime Museum 'Prins
Hendrick,' where the ship has been since 1930, has drawn a complete set of plans for the model. By permission of the Maritime Museum 'Prins Hendrik,' Rotterdam.

metals made up most of the cargoes loaded on vessels in Iberian
ports and along French Atlantic shores. England and the Low Countries still exported fine cloth, herring, beer, and finished goods to pay
for the raw materials that they imported from both the southern and
the northern edges of Atlantic Europe, but they relied upon Atlantic
galleys and other ships of the Genoese, Venetians, and Florentines to

A carrack of ca 1490 drawn in miniature to illustrate a
fifteenth-century edition of Flavius Josephus, *Jewish
Wars*. The fo′c′sle, crowded with men, is clearly a fighting platform. The hull appears very strong and the main
mast even more so, with its fighting top. Courtesy of
the Österreichische Nationalbibliothek, Vienna. Cod.
2538, fol. 109.

bring them alum and Mediterranean luxury products in return for
their woolens. The overall pattern of trade by 1498 had still not
changed very much, and the volume of goods reaching Atlantic
Europe from the Portuguese world of Africa and the offshore islands
or from the old Viking area of Iceland and Greenland was still rather
negligible in value or importance.

A large part of this northern bulk trade still was carried in seasonal
convoys of huge ships, though, since the population which consumed

these goods tended to be smaller than before, there was an incentive to save shipping costs by increasing the size of the vessels utilized. Thus, we find *cogs* of up to 500 tons being constructed, as well as similarly sized *hulks*, which competed with *cogs* in the Baltic trade, and even a composite *cog-hulk*-type vessel, which now made its appearance in these waters. Other sorts of vessels used in commerce, such as the *barges* and *balingers* of the Channel and the fishing *busses*, which Netherlanders used in the North Sea, also tended to become larger in order to save freight and labor costs. So, too, did those Atlantic fishing boats in which Bretons, Basques, and English fishermen sailed to Iceland and beyond. As was true of the Mediterranean during the late fourteenth and fifteenth centuries, economic pressures worked steadily to increase the size of most of the ships employed in Atlantic waters by the merchant and fishing community.

Much more important, however, than the increase in the size of merchant vessels in northern waters during these years was a series of technological changes in ship design, changes which amounted to a revolution on the seas and which resulted in the appearance of what might be called the full-rigged ship. The building traditions of the Mediterranean and the northern seas finally merged to produce new kinds of vessels which were better adapted to the oceans of the world than any which had preceded them.

The most important of these ships was known as the *carrack*. It was basically a modified *cog* or *hulk*, but one which was carvel-built in the frame-first Mediterranean fashion, and it carried initially two and finally three masts. It utilized a stern rudder of advanced design as well. Perhaps its most revolutionary features, however, were its bowsprit and its multiple sails, most of them square sails, but some triangular, which allowed for much more maneuverability in the open sea and on entering or leaving port. And finally it incorporated the fore and aft castles of the traditional *cog* into its design, and had special wales along the sides to protect the vessel while it was loading at a wharf.

There has been much discussion as to where the *carrack* originated, though it was probably somewhere between Santander and the North Sea, but it almost at once proved to be a remarkable sailor and a versatile one at that. It soon spread from Atlantic shores into the Mediterranean, where the Genoese began to build huge *carracks* especially suitable for carrying bulk cargoes like alum north or salt throughout the Middle Sea. Soon the Catalans and the Venetians found them useful and began construction of them as well. Somewhat more slowly, they spread from the North Sea into the Baltic, where, by the end of the fifteenth century, they began to replace the *hulks* that the Hansa was still building in Livonia and Prussia. One *carrack*, the *Santa Maria*, was the flagship used by Christopher Columbus in 1492, and they formed the fleet which Vasco da Gama sailed around Africa to South India. *Carracks* then, with later modifications, provided western Europeans with the vessels which they were to use over the next few centuries to dominate the seven seas of the world.

Though the *carrack* was the most important Atlantic ship type developed during this period, it had a competitor in the Portuguese *caravel*. This was a ship, originally of Islamic design, which was modified and used by Prince Henry the Navigator during initial Portuguese expansion along the West African coast and to the offshore islands. It was a carvel-built, narrow, two-masted vessel with lateen sails, which was unusually maneuverable and easy to operate along the dangerous shores which led to Guinea. And it made possible Portugal's success in exploiting her discoveries down to the last years of the fifteenth century. Columbus used two small *caravels* of 50 to 60 tons, the *Niña* and *Pinta*, in his first voyage west.

Still a third new type of vessel was the multimasted Netherlands-North Sea herring *buss*, which was invented or developed to fish in the North Sea during the fifteenth century and which may have been modified to fit the needs of North Atlantic fishermen. All of these vessels were, like the *carrack* and *caravel*, of frame-first construction and carvel-built and were thus economical to contruct as well as to operate at sea.

Still another aspect of this maritime technological revolution involves navigation. By the late fourteenth century—except in the Baltic where navigation with lead and line was the rule—this age saw improved compasses and portolan charts in use everywhere, along with complex sailing directions or *rutters*. Helpful, too, in navigation were the improved maps, which began to be produced in a number of localities—especially in Antwerp, Lisbon, and Seville. Even more remarkable is the way the Portuguese and their Italian captains made use of the Southern Cross for directional purposes when they ventured south of the Equator—using a knowledge of the stars that

The remains of the *Mary Rose*, begun 1509, rebuilt 1536. She sank
off Portsmouth in 1545 and was brought up and moved into a dock
in the same city in October 1982. A steel cradle supports the vessel
during recovery and while she is being sprayed with polyethelene-
glycol to preserve the timber. Artifacts found at the wreck site and
parts of the hull were removed for the lift from the seabed and are
housed separately. By permission of the *Mary Rose* Trust.

seems to have originated in the Indian Ocean. The same shipmasters
perfected latitude sailing over vast Atlantic distances until, by 1498,
they had become probably the world's most advanced navigators.

Two final questions, however, need to be answered. What effect
did all this technology have on warfare in the northern seas? And do
we find advances in naval tactics in the late fourteenth and fifteenth

Close-up of the *Mary Rose* covered with sprinklers to spray her
with fresh water. The beams, planking, and gun ports are clearly
shown. She capsized before being heavily engaged with the French
probably because she was top-heavy and because her gun ports were
too near the water line. Over 400 men drowned as she sank before a
dazed Henry VIII, who came to watch the sea battle.

centuries which match those of the previous period examined in the
last chapter? Our answers must be somewhat equivocal because
we have less evidence of naval conflict in northern waters during
these years, except for some French and Spanish raids in the 1380s on
English shores and the Portuguese seizure of Ceuta and other Atlantic
Moroccan ports between 1415 and 1420—in both cases without any

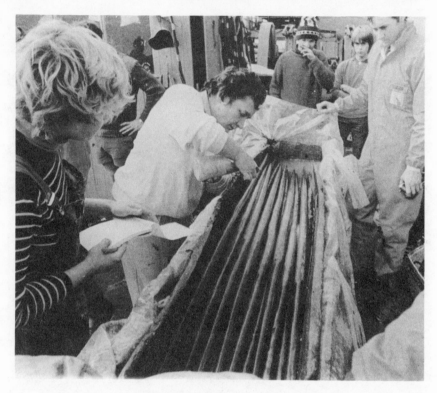

Some of the 250 longbows found on the *Mary Rose*, which sank in 1545 while maneuvering to engage the French. Their discovery not only provided weapons in such good condition that they could be draw-tested but also documented the continued importance of archers into the era of cannon. Courtesy of Margaret Rule and the *Mary Rose* Trust.

real opposition on the sea. Except for sporadic privateering in the narrow seas about the British Isles and in the Baltic, we cannot chart tactical naval advances here as we can in the more warlike Mediterranean.

Nevertheless, it is clear that the new full-rigged ships with their prominent forecastles and sterncastles were much more defensible than their predecessors. And although northern seamen were slow to use cannons, which for decades had been a prominent part of galley warfare in the Middle Sea, by the last years of the century, they had begun to do so. They placed them, however, amidships, so that they could fire through gun ports and be stable enough to make this part

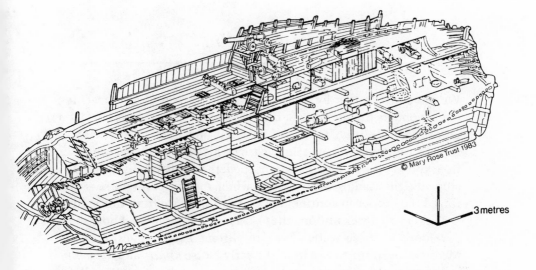

An interpretive reconstruction of the *Mary Rose* showing the interior deck arrangement. Note the air hatches on the top deck. Courtesy of the *Mary Rose* Trust.

of the vessel a natural gun platform. Down to the early sixteenth century, this use of guns in broadsides had not been tested in northern waters, but by that time, the *carrack* was recognized as a kind of floating fortress, which could use its multiple sails, its high degree of seaworthiness, the navigational skill of its crew, and its guns to dominate the wider world in the centuries to come.

Conclusion

WE HAVE NOTED that by 1500 western Europe was already reaching out beyond its Mediterranean-Black Sea and Atlantic shores to face a new oceanic destiny. This leads us to our final questions: What was the specific naval and maritime legacy which the medieval centuries from 500 to 1500 bequeathed to the modern world? Why is it useful to study the thousand years of history which took place on the seas that ringed the European continent? What can we learn from this study?

First of all, by examining these centuries, we learn just how ships developed in these waters from the *dromons* and *naves* of earlier Mediterranean times and from the early Norse *knarrs* and *longships* and from *keels*, *cogs*, and *hulks* of the north to become the galleys, *caravels*, and *carracks* of later times. We can, it is to be hoped, grasp that the warships and merchant ships of modern times, before the age of steel and steam, were essentially late medieval ships, only slightly modified from what they had become in the fifteenth century. What we are looking at, then, is really the origin of those vessels which made possible commerce and naval war as we know it from the modern age of sail. Furthermore, the use of crossbows and various kinds of catapults with which these early ships were equipped anticipates the way cannon and small arms were later employed and explains the tactics used already when, in the fifteenth century, guns became standard equipment on European ships at sea. In contrast, the equipment and tactics of ships used in ancient times seem totally archaic and irrelevant to us.

Equally important, we can learn about the evolution of naval tactics in an even broader sense when we examine these medieval centuries. During the earlier period, we are uncertain about what actually took place during naval conflict. We have no precise information, for instance, concerning exactly how the Arabs defeated the Byzantines in 655 at the Battle of the Masts, or how the latter, in 678 and 718, used Greek fire to destroy the vessels of their Muslim opponents during attacks on Constantinople. Nor do we have any clues as to how Alfred defeated the Danes on the sea in the 880s or how the Fatimids beat the Byzantines off Sicily in 975.

What does seem clear, however, is that down to 1100, naval battles took place in bays or quiet waters and probably were similar to encounters which took place on land. The crushing of the Syrian and Egyptian fleets of the Muslims in Atalia bay in 747, the Norse attacks on the Guadalquivir in 847, and the famous naval battle waged by Olaf Tryggvason at Svolder spring at once to mind.

By the twelfth century, we begin to have more precise information, and, for the first time, we begin to have data, which show that some naval battles were taking place in the open sea. The Venetian encounter with the Norman fleet off Durazzo in 1085, like their defeat of the Fatimid fleet off Tyre in 1128 and Richard the Lion-Hearted's encounter with Saladin's navy off Palestine in 1189, are examples of this new type of warfare. Now ships no longer simply served as fighting platforms on which land warfare methods could be employed at sea.

Once begun, the trend continued in the Mediterranean. Most of the important naval battles between the Genoese and the Venetians during their four naval wars of the thirteenth and fourteenth centuries took place in the open sea. So, too, did those which Roger Lauria fought against the Angevins and the French and those which the Catalans fought with the Genoese off Sardinia during these same centuries. The same is true of the battle between the Islamic Merinid naval forces and those of the Genoese and Portuguese in the Strait of Gibraltar in 1340. By now tactics used in naval battles had begun to approximate those found in modern naval wars.

Although northern Europe lagged far behind the Mediterranean in this respect, witness the battles of Damme and Sluys, fought a century apart, in which the French and the English slugged it out in port in the older fashion, we do at times find changes here, too. For instance, during the same period we have that battle off Sandwich in which the English admiral cut through a line of enemy ships in a way which would have made Admiral Blake proud of him. We also have the battle of Lags in 1263, fought by the Norwegians in the open sea off Scotland, and a number of similar engagements which occurred in the Baltic between the Hansa fleet and Scandinavian flotillas—all of which show the same kind of tactical naval advances.

Several other developments of a tactical sort which we can consider essentially modern began in these centuries, too. One was a system of convoying merchant ships. Such convoys began to be organized by the Genoese, Pisans, and Venetians in the twelfth century, perhaps copying their Islamic rivals in this respect. By the thirteenth century, the Italians and the Catalans regularly convoyed their merchant fleets on their annual voyages to the Levant or through the Strait of Gibraltar to the Channel and the North Sea—a practice which became so regular and accepted that it hardly needs comment.

By the thirteenth century, convoys were organized in northern waters to protect English ships trading with Gascony and Castilian vessels sailing through the Channel on their way to Bruges. The sorts of convoys which the Spanish were to employ in crossing the Atlantic with their great plate fleets in the sixteenth century and which saved Britain in two world wars were already in existence in European waters during the later Middle Ages.

Convoys were also frequently organized to address the matter of raiding or piracy, which were an aspect of naval tactics. Sometimes piracy was the only type of naval power available, as was the case with the Vandals or the Vikings. Sometimes it could be used as an advanced aspect of naval power, as it was in the case of the Arab pirate bases in the Mediterranean from the ninth to the eleventh century. The Mardaites who fought for Byzantium along the south coast of Asia Minor, the British and the French in the Channel during the later Middle Ages, and the Ottoman pirate fleets in the late fifteenth century also played such an advance role.

Piracy and privateering were also occasionally used by an inferior maritime power against superior naval forces that it could not deal with in open battle. Such was certainly the case with the Aegean pirates whom Michael Paleologus encouraged to attack the Venetians after 1261, with the Muslim corsairs of the Barbary coast and along Anatolian shores from the thirteenth century on, with the Wends and the Estonians of Livonia during the twelfth century, and with the Bretons during certain periods of the Hundred Years War. Such disparate experiences prove that raiding forces could be employed successfully, tactically speaking, in three ways: as the primary naval arm, as the cutting edge of a larger permanent naval establishment, or as the only answer to general naval inferiority.

And finally in tactical matters, we have the examples of systems of amphibious warfare, developed especially in the Mediterranean. As we have noted, Nicephorus Phocas's amphibious assault upon Crete represents an early and sophisticated example of such an operation, as does John Zimisces's destruction of the forces of Sviatoslav on the Danube a few years later. But we must regard the western Italian use of such warfare as even more remarkable, beginning with their late eleventh- and twelfth-century attacks against Palermo, Medhia, the Balearics, Almeria, and Tortosa in the west and against Syrian coastal towns in the Levant. Certainly, the amphibious operational masterpieces were the Venetian assaults on Constantinople during the Fourth Crusade, and those on Damietta during the Fifth and Sixth. Even later on, Italian navies continued to maintain considerable expertise in such operations. Witness their assault on Alexandria and Gallipoli in the 1360s and upon Smyrna a little later on. Nothing that was attempted along these lines in the Napoleonic Wars, the American Civil War or World War II surpasses medieval Europe's tactical abilities in this regard.

Finally, we need to sum up what we can learn from the medieval period concerning naval *strategy*. Again and again, we see naval power able to hold a far-flung empire together. We find it first when we examine the empire of Justinian and Heraclius and that of their Isaurian and Macedonian successors in the Mediterranean and Black seas. We see it also when we examine early Viking holdings in Ireland and Iceland and their links with Norway, and especially when we examine the maritime empire of King Canute.

Later on, the crusading states of Syria and Palestine furnish us with another excellent example of such a use of sea power, as does Venice's empire in *Romania* with its associated Frankish principalities in Greece. Hardly less impressive are the examples of Genoa's holdings in the same Aegean-Black Sea area or the domains of the House of Aragon in the western Mediterranean.

In the north and in the Atlantic region, we have the case of Livonian and Prussian holdings maintained by sea power exercised by Danes and Germans, as well as that of the empire of the English kings across the Channel in France and in Ireland for some four centuries after 1066. And finally, by the fifteenth century, we have the remarkable Portuguese overseas empire stretching down the coast of Africa from Ceuta to Angola and out into the Atlantic to the Cape Verdes and the Azores. The maritime empires which in modern times have become the hallmark of Europe after 1500 are foreshadowed again and again during the Middle Ages.

Finally, in dealing with strategic matters, we have certain

examples of a close connection between naval power and economic development, especially development related to foreign trade and maritime expansion—what might, in short, be called a naval-maritime industrial complex comparable to aspects of our modern world. In the Middle Sea, in a sense, the success of the revived Empire of Byzantium during the sixth and seventh centuries was due to the interrelationship between the advanced trading and industrial cities of its Syrian and Greek areas in the eastern Mediterranean and its western naval and imperial conquests. The same close interrelationship existed down to 1200 between the financial, industrial, commercial, and maritime aspects of the Islamic Mediterranean and its naval successes.

From the thirteenth century onward, it was this same interaction between naval power and economic development which characterized the world of the Italians and then of the Provençals and of the Catalans, who were able to combine new and expanding financial horizons with maritime innovations to form a basis for their new naval strength. The failure of Byzantium to foster such interaction caused it to fall behind the Arabs on the sea in the ninth century, and the Islamic Mediterranean empire steadily declined before the Latin west from the time of the Crusades until the rise of the Ottomans for the same reason.

In the northern seas and in western Atlantic waters, the same thing is true. There was a close relationship between the sea power of the Vikings and their commercial interests, a feature which distinguished them from their fifth-century German predecessors. When first the Anglo-Saxons and then the Hanseatic Germans replaced the Scandinavians as the leading naval powers of the north, a close interrelationship between commercial, financial, and naval strength is again apparent, as it is also in the cases of England between 1000 and 1350, the Hanseatic League, and Portugal.

These pages have shown, we trust, the limitations inherent in naval power, considered in a historical setting. It is clear that the Byzantine naval empire of Justinian and his successors found it especially difficult to translate its naval strength into victories over Lombards, Carolingians, and the Ottos on the mainland of Italy, over Slavs and Bulgars in the interior of the Balkans, over Arabs in Syria and Egypt, or over Turks in the center of Asia Minor.

Similarly, in the Latin west, nothing is more revealing than the failure of the crusading states of Syria and Palestine to translate their overwhelming sea power into strength in the interior, as shown by the failure of the Second, Third, Fifth, and Sixth Crusades. Who can help but be impressed by a similar failure of the Latins in Byzantium after 1204 when they faced Greeks or Bulgars in interior areas. And after 1250, when Latin fleets ranged the Mediterranean and Black seas unchallenged, the Seljuk and Ottoman Turks and the Mamluks were nevertheless remarkably successful in maintaining their authority over their own realms.

A similar situation is revealed when we examine northern European regions. Viking sea power was unable to hold Frisia, defeat Alfred the Great in England, or subdue Ireland during the years of their greatest naval preponderance. Nor was King John's navy able to prevent his losing northern France to Philip Augustus. And English sea power could not assure that Henry V's successors hold their French possessions later on. Even in the distant Baltic, the failure of the Teutonic knights to advance into the interior in the face of Lithuanian or Polish opposition reveals another limitation of sea power during these years.

A number of lessons, then, emerge from an examination of naval power during the Middle Ages. One discovers how modern ships came to be developed and armed for conflict on the sea. One can discern the beginnings of real tactics in naval battles fought on the open ocean. One can also see the development of amphibious warfare and of raiding activities of various sorts, as well as of convoy systems, which were a response to such raids. In the matter of overall strategy, one can see how sea power would be used to maintain overseas empires and how it could be combined with financial, commercial, and maritime interests.

Finally, the reader of these pages needs to grasp the limitations of naval and maritime power which again and again have been revealed in these pages. Our own nation, which stands out as a leading proponent of sea power, would be especially wise to consider these limitations before other crises, such as those which have taken place in Vietnam, Iran, and Lebanon, occur to remind us. For it remains true that the nation which does not learn from the past is doomed to repeat it.

Bibliographical Note

There is no comprehensive introductory bibliography for medieval naval and maritime history. John S. Illsley of the University College of North Wales has computerized a bibliography of nautical archaeology and history which may be available soon. The standard introduction is R.G. Albion, *Maritime and Naval History: An Annotated Bibliography* 4th ed. (Mystic, Conn., 1972). *The International Medieval Bibliography* (Minneapolis, 1967–) is also helpful. Also useful are the eight volumes edited by M. Mollat from 1957 to 1970 of the International Conference on Maritime History, *Travaux du Colloque International d'Histoire Maritime* (Paris, 1957–70). The Commission Internationale d'histoire Maritime has published the proceedings of the 1980 Bucharest conference, *Gens de Mer en Société*, edited by P. Adam (Paris, 1981). The commission meets every five years with the International Congress of Historical Sciences.

The principal journals in the field are the best means of keeping abreast of current developments. These include: *The American Neptune* (Salem, Mass., 1941–); *Handels–og Søfartsmuseum Pa Kronborg, Arbog* (Helsinor, 1942–); *The International Journal of Nautical Archaeology and Underwater Exploration* (London, 1972–); *Marine Academie von België, Mededelingen* (Antwerp, 1950–), *The Mariner's Mirror* (Cambridge, 1911–); *Sjøfartshistorisk Arbok* (Norway) (Bergen, 1965–); *Sjøhistorisk Arsbok* (Stockholm, 1940–). There are many maritime museums which publish important papers and monographs, including the National Maritime Museum, Greenwich, England. Also useful is Helmut Pemsel, *A History of War at Sea*, revised edition (Annapolis, 1977), which is a chronological outline and historical atlas. On historical geography, N. Pounds, *An Historical Geography of Medieval Europe*, 450 B.C.–A.D. 1330 (Cambridge, 1978) is recommended.

There are several military histories of note: C.W.C. Oman, *The Art of War in the Middle Ages*, 2 vols. (London, 1924); P. Contamine, *La Guerre au Moyen Age* (Paris, 1980), which has a good bibliography; and J.F. Verbruggen, *The Art of Warfare in Western Europe during the Middle Ages (from the Eighth Century to 1340)* (original ed., Brussels, 1954; English translation, Amsterdam, 1976).

For the fast growing subject of underwater archeology the following are suggested and cover a number of chronological and geographical areas. For a general introduction, G.F. Bass, editor, *A History of Seafaring based on Underwater Archaeology* (New York, 1972) and his *Archaeology Underwater* (New York, 1966), and *Archaeology Beneath the Sea* (New York, 1975). Honor Frost, *Under the Mediterranean* (London, 1963) is by another pioneer in the field. Keith Muckelroy published two useful books: *Archeology Under Water, An Atlas of the World's Submerged Sites* (New York, 1980),

171

and a review of the state of the field in *Maritime Archaeology* (Cambridge, 1978). Joan du Plat Taylor edited *Marine Archaeology* (London, 1965), a summary of Mediterranean projects over a sixty-year period. See also the collected papers in D.J. Blackman, editor, *Marine Archaeology*, Colston papers, no. 23 (London, 1973). Another work by a pioneer in the field is Peter Throckmorton's *Shipwrecks and Archaeology* (Boston, 1970). The National Maritime Museum in Greenwich, England has recently produced a series of introductory works under the general editorship of Basil Greenhill including: Sean McGrail, *The Ship. Rafts, Boats and Ships from Prehistoric Times to the Medieval Era* (London, 1981); John Morrison, *The Ship. Long Ships and Round Ships, Warfare and Trade in the Mediterranean, 3,000 B.C. – 500 A.D.* (London, 1980); Alan McGowan, *The Ship. Tiller and Whipstaff, The Development of the Sailing Ship, 1400–1700* (London, 1981).

Special attention should be given to the *International Journal of Nautical Archaeology and Underwater Exploration*, but see also *Progress in Underwater Science*, annual report of the Underwater Association (London, Pentech Press). Current work at the Institute of Nautical Archaeology at Texas A&M University is noted in its *Newsletter*. Several recent articles do much to encourage interest: G.F. Bass, "Underwater Archaeology: Key to History's Warehouse," *National Geographic Magazine*, 124 (1963), pp. 138–56; his "New Tools for Underwater Archaeology," ibid., 134 (1968), pp. 403–23. The recent discovery and recovery of the *Mary Rose* is beautifully illustrated in M. Rule's "Henry VIII's Lost Warship," ibid., 163 (May 1983), pp. 646–675.

For the technical aspects of archeological work, see Philip Barker, *The Techniques of Archaeological Excavation* (London, 1977) and the solid introduction by P.J. Fowler, *Approaches to Archaeology* (New York, 1977). An illustrated survey of recent evidence is B. Greenhill, *Archaeology of the Boat* (London, 1976). Two basic works are A. Jal's *Archéologie Navale*, 2 vols. (Paris, 1840) and *Glossaire nautique. Répertoire polyglotte de terms de marine anciens et modernes*, 2 vols. (Paris, 1848–50), now being revised: *Nouveau Glossaire Nautique*, Editions du Centre national de la Recherche scientifique (Paris, 1970 –, vols. A–E completed in 1983.

One instance of the remarkable discoveries made in this field is the Athlit ram, the first intact ram to be excavated. The fourth century B.C. bronze ram was discovered in 1980 in the Sea of Athlit off the coast of northern Israel. See J.R. Steffy, "The Athlit Ram. A Preliminary Investigation of its Structure," *Mariner's Mirror*, 69 (August 1983), pp. 229–47. Another fascinating example is the discovery of an eleventh century vessel wrecked off Turkey with Byzantine and Islamic artifacts: G.F. Bass, "Glass Treasure from the Aegean," *National Geographic* 153, 6 (June 1978), pp. 768–93. On related topics see J.R. Steffy, "Nautical Archaeology: Construction Techniques of Ancient Ships," *Naval Engineers Journal*, 87 (1975), pp. 85–90. An introduction to the important area of conservation and future prospects of deep water discoveries is Willard Bascom, *Deep Water, Ancient Ships* (New York, 1976).

Illustrations of ships are very important sources in the absence of ship remains. The most comprehensive work is F. Möll, *Das Schiff in der Bilden-*

den Kunst (Bonn, 1929), but the illustrations are poor. Also of use are: H. Ewe, *Shiffe auf Siegeln* (Bielefeld, 1971); G.F. Bass, ed., *A History of Seafaring Based on Underwater Archaeology* (London, 1972); B. Landstrom, *The Ship* (London, 1961) for drawings based on early ship representations; L. Casson, *Illustrated History of Ships and Boats* (New York, 1964); R. and R.C. Anderson, *The Sailing Ship* (London, 1926). The work of Christiane Villain-Gandossi is of special note: "La Navire medieval à travers les miniatures des manuscrits français," in *The Archaeology of Medieval Ships and Harbors in Northern Europe*, S. McGrail, editor (Greenwich, 1979), pp. 195–225; "Terminologie de l'Appereil de gouverne (ixe–xviiie siècles)," *Archaeonautica* 2 (1978), pp. 281–309; see her collected essays in *La Méditerranée aux xiie–xvie siècles: relations maritimes, diplomatiques et commerciales* (London: Variorum Reprints, 1983).

Suggestions for Further Reading

CHAPTER I.
THE LATE ROMAN WORLD TO A.D. 500

The basic studies are L. Casson, *The Ancient Mariners* (New York, 1959) and *Ships and Seamanship in the Ancient World* (Princeton, 1971), and see his *Travel in the Ancient World* (London, 1974). C.G. Starr, *The Roman Imperial Navy, 31 B.C. to 324 A.D.*, 2d ed. (Cambridge, 1966); and J. Rougé, *La marine dans l'antiquité* (Paris, 1975), English translation by S. Frazer entitled *Ships and Fleets of the Ancient Mediterranean* (Middletown, Conn., 1981). See also R.C. Anderson, *Oared Fighting Ships* (London, 1962).

For the later period, see A.R. Lewis, "Mediterranean Maritime Commerce: A.D. 300–1100, Shipping and Trade," in *The Sea and Medieval Civilizations* (London: Variorum Reprints, 1978), ch. 12; and *The Northern Seas, A.D. 300–1100* (Princeton, 1958), pp. 1–109. For the Vandals see C. Courtois, *Les Vandales de l'Afrique* (Paris, 1954). And for Roman ships and harbors, P. Throckmorton, "Romans on the Sea," pp. 65–86, and J.W. Shaw, "Greek and Roman Harbourworks," pp. 87–112, in G. Bass, ed., *A History of Seafaring Based on Underwater Archaeology* (London, 1972), and especially R.W. Unger, *The Ship in the Medieval Economy* (Montreal, 1980), pp. 33–40. An important article is R.H. Dolley, "The Warships of the Late Roman Empire," *Journal of Roman Studies*, 38 (1948), pp. 47–53.

The following works are often more specialized, but are important for this period: J.H. D'Arms and E.C. Kopff, *The Seaborne Commerce of Ancient Rome* (Rome, 1980); J.H. D'Arms, *Romans on the Bay of Naples* (Cambridge, Mass., 1970); M. Cary and E. Warmington, *The Ancient Explorers* (New York, 1929); E. Warmington, *Commerce between the Roman Empire and India* (Cambridge, 1928); J. Rougé, *Recherches sur l'organisation du commerce maritime en méditerranée sous l'empire romain* (Paris, 1966); W.L. Rodgers, *Naval Warfare Under Oars, 4th to 16th Centuries* (Annapolis, 1940) and *Greek and Roman Naval Warfare* (Annapolis, 1939); J.M. Carter, *The Battle of Actium* (London, 1970); R. Custance, *War at Sea: Modern Theory and Ancient Practice* (London, 1918; reprint 1970); W.W. Tarn, *Hellenistic Military and Naval Developments* (Cambridge, 1920); H.A. Ormerod, *Piracy in the Ancient World* (Liverpool, 1924); for an archeological survey, see A.J. Parker, *Ancient Shipwrecks of the Mediterranean and Roman Provinces*, British Archaeological Reports (Oxford, 1980); for law, Walter Ashburner, *The Rhodian Sea Law* (Oxford, 1909); C. Torr, *Ancient Ships* (Cambridge, 1895); for the Alexandria-Rome grain ships, see G. Rickman, *The Corn Supply of Ancient Rome* (Oxford, 1980), and L. Casson, "The *Isis* and her Voyage," *Transactions of the American Philological Association* 81 (1950), pp. 43–56; "The Size of Ancient Merchant Ships," *Studi in onore di Aristide*

Calderini e Roberto Paribeni (Milan, 1956), I, pp. 231–38; "New Light on Ancient Rigging and Boatbuilding," *American Neptune* 24 (1964), pp. 81–94, and his "Speed under Sail of Ancient Ships," *Transactions of the American Philological Association* 82 (1959), pp. 136–48. For hull preservation, L. Basch, "The Metal Sheathing of Roman Warships," *Mariner's Mirror* 65 (February, 1979), pp. 29–36.

CHAPTER II.
BYZANTINE NAVAL POWER AND SHIPPING, 500–1291

The basic studies are A.R. Lewis, *Naval Power and Trade in the Mediterranean, A.D. 500–1100* (Princeton, 1951) and H. Ahrweiler, *Byzance et la Mer* (Paris, 1966). Also useful are H. Antoniades-Bibicou, *Etudes d'histoire maritime de Byzance* (Paris, 1966); C.M. Brand, *Byzantium Confronts the West, 1180–1204* (Cambridge, Mass., 1965); G. Bratianu, *La Mer Noire des origines à la conquête ottomane* (Munich, 1869); H. Ahrweiler, "L'escale dans le monde byzantin" in *Recueils de la Société Jean Bodin* 32 (1974), pp. 162–78; R.H. Dolley, "Naval Tactics in the Heyday of the Byzantine Thalassocracy" in *Atti del' VIIIe Congresso di Studi Bizantini* I (Rome, 1953), pp. 324–339, and A.R. Lewis, "Byzantine Lightweight Solidi and Trade to the North Sea and Baltic" in *The Sea and Medieval Civilizations* (London, 1978), pp. 131–55.

Useful for naval construction and technology is the first complete report on the excavation of an early Mediterranean ship, G.F. Bass, F.H. Van Doorninck, et al., *Yassi Ada: A Seventh Century Byzantine Shipwreck* (College Station, Texas, 1982). See also: F. Van Doorninck, "Byzantium, Mistress of the Sea, 300–641," in G.F. Bass, ed., *A History of Seafaring*, pp. 133–58. A ship which marks the change to frame-first construction is discussed in G.F. Bass and F.H. Van Doorninck, "An 11th c. Shipwreck at Serçe Liman, Turkey," *International Journal of Nautical Archaeology* 7, 2 (1978), pp. 119–32 and in J.R. Steffy, "The Reconstruction of the 11th Century Serçe Liman Vessel," ibid. 11, 1 (1982), pp. 13–34. For warfare at sea: J.R. Partington, *A History of Greek Fire and Gunpowder* (Cambridge, 1961). For piracy in the thirteenth century Aegean, see G. Morgan, "The Venetian Claims Commission of 1278" in *Byzantinische Zeitschrift* 69 (1976), pp. 411–437.

Constantine Porphyrogenitus, author of *De Caerimoniis*, is an excellent source. See A. Toynbee, *Constantine Porphyrogenitus and his World* (London, 1973), ch. 7 on the navy. Also note G. Bass, "A Byzantine Trading Venture," *Scientific American* 225 (1971), pp. 23–33 on a seventh century vessel. For navies: J.B. Bury, "The Naval Policy of the Roman Empire to the Ninth Century," in *Centenario della Nascita de Michele Amari* (Palermo, 1910), pp. 21–34 and L. Bréhier, "La marine de Byzance du VIIIe au xie siècle," *Byzantion* 19 (1949), pp. 1–16. For waterborne transport, see A.C. Leighton, *Transport and Communication in Early Medieval Europe, A.D. 500–1100* (Newton Abbot, England, 1972), ch. 3.

CHAPTER III.
MUSLIM NAVAL AND MARITIME POWER IN
THE MEDITERRANEAN, 651–1498

Basic studies of the earlier period are A.R. Lewis, *Naval Power and Trade;* E. Eickhoff, *Seekrieg und Seepolitik zwischen Islam und Abendland: Das Mittelmeer unter Byzantinischer und Arabischer Hegemonie* (650–1040) (Berlin, 1966); and A. Fahmy, *Muslim Sea Power in the Eastern Mediterranean from the Seventh to the Tenth Century* (Cairo, 1966). For economy and shipping, see S.D. Goitein, *A Mediterranean Society. The Jewish Communities of the Arab World as Portrayed in the Documents of the Cairo Geniza,* 3 vols. (Berkeley, 1967–71). For conditions of navigation, A.R. Lewis, "Mediterranean Maritime Commerce: A.D. 300–1100, Shipping and Trade," *Settimane di studio del Centro italiano di Studi Sull'alto Medioevo* XXV (Spoleto, 1978), pp. 481–501.

For the later Middle Ages in the western Mediterranean, see R. Letourneau, *The Almohad Movement in North Africa in the Twelfth and Thirteenth Centuries* (Princeton, 1969); R. Brunschvig, *La Berbérie Orientale sous les Hafsids,* 2 vols. (Paris, 1947); R. Arié, *L'Espagne Musulmane au temps de Nasarides (1232–1492)* (Paris, 1973); and A. Hess, *The Forgotten Frontier, A History of the Sixteenth Century Ibero-African Frontier* (Chicago, 1978), pp. 1–44.

For the same period in the eastern Mediterranean, see A. Ehrenkreutz, *Saladin* (Albany, 1972); D. Ayalon, *Gunpowder and Firearms in the Mamluk Kingdom* (London, 1956) and *Studies on the Mamluks of Egypt (1250–1517),* (London: Variorum Reprints, 1977); A.C. Hess, "The Evolution of the Ottoman Seaborne Empire in the Age of Oceanic Discoveries, 1453–1525" in *American Historical Review* 75 (December 1970), pp. 1892–1919; and K. Setton, *The Papacy and the Levant,* II, *The Fifteenth Century* (Philadelphia, 1978). Note also G. Hourani, *Arab Seafaring in the Indian Ocean in Ancient and Early Medieval Times* (Princeton, 1951); A.R. Lewis, "Les Marchands dans l'ocean indien," *Revue d'histoire économique et sociale* 56, 4 (1976), pp. 441–75; S.D. Goitein, "Medieval Tunisia: The Hub of the Mediterranean," in *Studies in Islamic History and Institutions,* ed. S.D. Goitein (Leiden, 1968); M. Lombard, "Arsenaux et Bois de Marine dans la Méditerranée Musulmane, VII–XIe siècles," in M. Mollat, ed., *La Navire et l'economie maritime du moyen age au XVIIIe siècle principalement en Méditerranée* (Paris, 1958), pp. 53–99.

CHAPTER IV
LATIN WESTERN NAVAL POWER AND SHIPPING
IN THE MEDITERRANEAN, 800–1498

Basic works are C. Manfroni, *Storia de la marina italiana,* 3 vols. (Rome, 1897–1902); J. Hocquet, *Voliers et commerce en Mediterranée,* 1200–1650 (Lille, 1979); and K. Setton, *The Papacy and the Levant,* 1204–1571, 2 vols.

(1976–78). For Amalfi: A. Citarelli, "The Relations of Amalfi with the Arab World before the Crusades" in *Speculum*, 42 (April 1967), pp. 299–316; for Norman Sicily: E. Jamison, *Admiral Eugenius of Sicily* (London, 1957); for Genoa: R.S. Lopez, *Su e giu per la Storia de Genova* (Genoa, 1975); E.H. Byrne, *Genoese Shipping in the Twelfth and Thirteenth Centuries* (Cambridge, Mass., 1930); G. Bratianu, *Recherches sur le Commerce Genois dans la Mer Noire au XIIIe Siècle* (Paris, 1929); for Venice: F.C. Lane, *Venice, A Maritime Republic* (Baltimore, 1973) and the collected essays in *Venice and History* (Baltimore, 1966); J. Heers, *Gênes au XVe Siècle* (Paris, 1961); P. Argenti, *The Occupation of Chios by the Genoese and their Administration of the Island, 1346–1566* (Cambridge, 1958); A. Wiel, *The Navy of Venice* (London, 1910); J. Sottas, *Les Messageres maritimes de Venise au XIVe et XVe siècles* (Paris, 1938); D. Queller, *The Fourth Crusade* (Philadelphia, 1978); D. Chambers, *The Imperial Age of Venice, 1380–1580* (London, 1970); and F. Thiriet, *La Romanie Venetienne au Moyen Âge* (Paris, 1959); for the Knights of Rhodes: A. Luttrell, *The Hospitalers in Cyprus, Rhodes, Greece and the West 1200–1571* (London: Variorum Reprints, 1978).

For Catalonia, Aragon, and Castile: C.E. Dufourcq, *L'Espagne Catalane et le Maghreb aux XIIIe et XIVe siècles* (Paris, 1966) and *La Vie quotidienne dans les ports méditerranéens au Moyen Age (Provence-Languedoc-Catalogne)* (Paris, 1975); C. Carrère, *Barcelone, centre économique à la époque des difficultés (1380–1462)* (Paris, 1967); and A. Hess, *The Forgotten Frontier*, pp. 1–89. For southern France: C. de La Roncière, *Histoire de la marine française*, 5 vols., 3rd ed. (Paris, 1909–32), I; and M. Mollat, *Les affaires de Jacques Coeur*, 2 vols. (Paris, 1952–53); and C. Farrère, *Histoire de la marine française* (Paris, 1962), pp. 1–98. Note also, W. Cohn, *Die Geschichte der Sizilischen Flotte unter der Regierung Friedrichs II* (1926). Note also F. Pérez-Embid and F. Padrón, *Bibliografia española de historia maritima (1932–1962)* (Seville, 1970).

For ship construction and naval technology: B. Kreutz, "Ships, Shipping and the Implications of Change in the Early Medieval Mediterranean," *Viator* 7 (1976), pp. 79–109; A. Jal, *Archeologie Navale*, 2 vols. (Paris, 1840); R.C. Anderson, "Italian Naval Architecture about 1450" in *Mariners Mirror* 11(1925); F.C. Lane, *Navires et constructeurs à Venise pendant la Renaissance* (Paris, 1965) a revision of the original English edition, Baltimore, 1934; C. Cipolla, *Guns and Sails in the Early Phase of European Expansion, 1400–1700* (New York, 1965); E. Scandurra, "The Maritime Republics: Medieval and Renaissance Ships in Italy" in G. Bass, ed., *A History of Seafaring*, pp. 205–224; J.E. Dotson, "Merchant and Naval Influences on Galley Design at Venice and Genoa in the Fourteenth Century," in C.L. Symonds, ed., *New Aspects of Naval History* (Annapolis, 1981), pp. 20–32; his "Jal's Nef X and Genoese Naval Architecture in the 13th Century," *Mariner's Mirror* 59 (May 1973), pp. 161–70; J.R. Steffy, "The Reconstruction of the 11th Century Sirçe Liman Vessel," *International Journal of Nautical Archaeology* 11 (1982), pp. 13–34; J.H. Pryor, "The Naval Architecture of Crusader Transport Ships," *Mariner's Mirror* 90 (May 1984), pp. 171–219 and (August 1984); R. Bastard de Péré, "Navires Méditerranéens du temps de Saint Louis," *Revue d'histoire économique et sociale* 50 (1972), pp. 327–56.

Important for calculating carrying capacity and cargoes is F.C. Lane, "Tonnages, Medieval and Modern," *Economic History Review*, 2nd ser., 17 (1964–65), pp. 213–33. On transport for war see J.H. Pryor, "Transportation of Horses by Sea during the Era of the Crusades," *Mariner's Mirror* 68 (February 1982), pp. 9–27 and (May 1982), pp. 103–26. On crusading warfare see D.P. Waley, "Combined Operations in Sicily, A.D. 1060–1078," *Papers of the British School at Rome*, n.s. 9 (1954), pp. 118–25; R.C. Smail, *Crusading Warfare (1097–1193)* (Cambridge, 1956); K. Settron, gen. ed., *The History of the Crusades* (1962 ff.); M. Mollat, "Problèmes navals de l'histoire des croisades," *Cahiers de civilisation médiévale* 10 (1967), pp. 345–59 and J.F. Guilmartin, *Gunpowder and Galleys. Changing Technology and Mediterranean Warfare at Sea* (Cambridge, 1974); "The Early Provision of Artillery Armament on Mediterranean War Galleys," *Mariner's Mirror* 59 (August 1973), pp. 257–80. Documents which relate to shipping in this period are found in R.S. Lopez and I.W. Raymond, *Medieval Trade in the Mediterranean World* (New York, 1955). Note also Eliyahu Ashtor's essays in *Studies in the Levantine Trade in the Middle Ages* (London, 1978). For the life of a merchant, F.C. Lane, *Andrea Barbarigo, Merchant of Venice, 1418–1449* (Baltimore, 1944).

CHAPTER V.
IRISH, FRISIANS, AND VIKINGS IN
THE NORTHERN SEAS, 500–1066

The basic studies are: A.R. Lewis, *The Northern Seas*, pp. 94–454; and R.W. Unger, *The Ship in the Medieval Economy*, pp. 55–117. For Celtic seafaring, see: J. Morris, *The Age of Arthur* (New York, 1974); and L. Fleuriot, *Les origines de la Bretagne. L'émigration* (Paris, 1980). For the Frisians: D. Jellema, "Frisian Trade in the Dark Ages" in *Speculum* 30 (January 1955), pp. 15–36.

A number of excellent books on the Vikings are in print. Among them are G. Jones, *A History of the Vikings* (Oxford, 1968); P. Sawyer, *The Age of the Vikings* (London, 1977) and *Kings and Vikings* (London, 1982); P. Foote and D. Wilson, *The Viking Achievement* (London, 1970). For Scandinavian voyages to Greenland and North America, see G. Jones, ed., *The Norse Atlantic Saga* (London, 1964).

For ship construction, see V. Fenwick, ed., *The Graveney Boat*, British Archaeological Report, 53 (Oxford, 1978) and *Boat Finds in Britain*, National Maritime Museum, monograph no. 6 (Greenwich, 1972); A.W. Brøgger and H. Shetelig, *The Viking Ships* (Oslo, 1951); and O. Crumlin-Pedersen, *The Viking Ships of Roskilde* (London, Maritime Monographs and Reports, No. 1, 1970). A.E. Christensen, "Scandinavian Ships from the Earliest Times to the Vikings" and O. Crumlin-Pedersen, "The Vikings and the Hanseatic Merchants," in *A History of Seafaring Based on Underwater Archaeology*, G. Bass, ed. (London, 1972), pp. 159–80 and 181–204; O. Olsen and O. Crumlin-Pedersen, "The Skuldelev Ships," *Acta Archaeologica* 29 (1958), pp. 161–75;

38 (1967), pp. 73–174 and see their well-illustrated *Five Viking Ships from Roskilde Fjord*, trans. B. Bluestone (Copenhagen, 1978); O. Crumlin-Pedersen, "Viking Shipbuilding and Seamanship," *Proceedings of the 8th Viking Congress*, eds. H. Bekker-Nielsen, P. Foote, O. Olsen (Odense, 1981), pp. 271–86 suggests a pattern for the evolution of northern ships. D. Ellmers, *Frühmittelalterliche Handelsschiffahrt in Mittel-Nordeuropa* (Neumünster, 1972), catalogues the ship finds of northern Europe. See also, A.E. Christensen, "Viking Age Ships and Shipbuilding," *Norwegian Archaeological Review* 15, 1–2 (1982), pp. 19–28, and his "Boatbuilding Tools and the Process of Learning," in O. Hasslof, et al., eds., *Ships and Shipyards, Sailors and Fishermen* (Copenhagen, 1972), pp. 235–59; G.J. Marcus, "The Evolution of the Knörr," *Mariner's Mirror*, 41 (May 1955), pp. 115–22. For seaworthiness, S. McGrail and E. McKee, *The Building and Trials of the Replica of an Ancient Boat: The Gokstad Faering*, 2 parts, National Maritime Museum Monographs and Reports, no. 11 (Greenwich, 1974). See also the views of G.A. Cottell, "The Gokstad Ship: Some New Theories Concerning the Purposes of its Constructional Features," *Mariner's Mirror* 70 (May 1984), pp. 129–42.

For the Nydam ship see H. Akerlund, *Nydamskeppen* (Goteborg, 1963); G.J. Marcus, "The Nydam Craft and the Anglo-Saxon Invasions," *Mariner's Mirror* 41 (February 1955), pp. 66 and related works, H. Marwick, "Naval Defence in Norse Scotland," *Scottish Historical Review* 28 (1949), pp. 1–11; E.G. Bowen, *Britain and the Western Seaways* (London, 1972).

The ship found at Sutton Hoo has received much attention: R.P. Bruce-Mitford, *The Sutton Hoo Ship Burial*, 2 vols. (London, 1975–78); and *The Sutton Hoo Ship Burial: A Handbook*, 3rd ed. (London, 1979).

CHAPTER VI.
THE AGE OF THE ENGLISH AND THE
HANSA IN THE NORTH, 1066–1377

The basic studies again are: R.W. Unger, *The Ship in the Medieval Economy*, pp. 119–213; and A.R. Lewis, *The Northern Seas*, pp. 455–489. For warfare see P. Contamine, *Guerre, état et société à la fin du Moyen Age* (Paris, 1972).

A number of important studies exist dealing with English naval forces. Some of the more recent are: F.W. Brooks, *The English Naval Forces*, 1199–1272 (Manchester, 1932); T.J. Runyan, "Ships and Mariners in Later Medieval England" in *Journal of British Studies* 16 (Spring 1977), pp. 1–17; "Mariners and the Law of the Sea in Later Medieval England" in *Gens de mer en société*, Commission Internationale d'histoire maritime, ed. P. Adam (Paris, 1981), pp. 1–12; "Merchantmen to Men-of-War in Medieval England," in *New Aspects of Naval History*, ed. C.L. Symonds (Annapolis, 1981), pp. 33–40; M. Prestwich, *War, Politics and Finance under Edward I* (London, 1972), pp. 137–50; H.J. Hewitt, *The Organization of War under Edward III*, 1338–1362 (Manchester, 1966); J.S. Kepler, "The Effects of the Battle of Sluys upon the Administration of English Naval Impressment," *Speculum* 48 (January 1973), pp. 70 – 77; A.E. Prince, "The Army and the Navy," in *The English Government at*

Work, 1327–1336, eds. J.F. Willard and W.A. Morris, 3 vols. (Cambridge, Mass., 1940–50), I, 376–93; and J. Sherborne, "The English Navy: Shipping and Manpower, 1369–1389" in *Past and Present* 37 (1967); "The Battle of La Rochelle and the War at Sea, 1372–5," in *Bulletin of the Institute of Historical Research*, 42 (May 1969); H.J. Hewitt, *The Black Prince's Expedition*, 1355–1357 (Manchester, 1958); J.J. McCusker, "The Wine Prise and Medieval Mercantile Shipping," *Speculum* 41 (April 1966), pp. 279–96; C.J. Ford, "Piracy or Policy: The Crisis in the Channel, 1400–1403," *Transactions of the Royal Historical Society*, 5th ser., 29 (1979), 63–78; the studies of C.F. Richmond, "The Keeping of the Seas during the Hundred Years War: 1422–1440," *History*, 49 (October 1964), pp. 283–298; "English Naval Power in the Fifteenth Century," *History* 52 (February 1967), pp. 1–15 and C.F. Richmond, "The War at Sea," in K. Fowler, ed., *The Hundred Years War* (London, 1971), pp. 96–121. Two comprehensive studies are: W.L. Clowes, et al., *The Royal Navy, A History from the Earliest Times to the Present*, 7 vols. (London, 1897–1903) and N.H. Nicolas, *History of the Royal Navy*, 2 vols., (London, 1847). See also: R. Hargreaves, *The Narrow Seas* (London, 1959); A.Z. Freeman, "A Moat Defensive: The Coast Defense Scheme of 1295," *Speculum* 42 (July, 1967), 442–62, Henry L. Cannon, "The Battle of Sandwich and Eustace the Monk," *English Historical Review*, 27 (October 1912, pp. 649–70; W.S. Reid, "Sea-Power in the Anglo-Scottish War, 1296–1328," *Mariner's Mirror* 46 (February 1960), pp. 7–23; C. Platt, *Medieval Southampton* (London, 1973). For commerce see E. Carus-Wilson, *Medieval Merchant Adventurers* (London, 1954) and with O. Coleman, *England's Export Trade*, 1275–1547 (Oxford, 1963).

For Gascony and its trade: M.W. Labarge, *Gascony, England's First Colony*, 1204–1453 (London, 1980); M.K. James, *Studies in the Medieval Wine Trade*, ed. E.M. Veale (Oxford, 1971), an important collection of essays; and Y. Renouard, "L'exportation des vins Gascons" in *Histoire de Bordeaux* III (Bordeaux, 1965). M. Gouron, *L'Amiraute de Guyenne* (Paris, 1938). Also for France and the Atlantic trade: J. Craeybeckx, *Un grand commerce de importation: les vins France au anciens Pays-Bas (XIIIᵉ–XVIᵉ siècles)* (Paris, 1959); N.J.M. Kerling, *Commercial Relations with Holland and Zeeland with England from the late 13th Century to the Close of the Middle Ages* (Leiden, 1954); R.W. Unger, "The Netherlands Herring Fishery in the Middle Ages: The False Legend of the Willem Beukels of Biervliet," *Viator* 9 (1978), 355–56.

On warfare see: M. Mollat, "Les marins et la guerre sur mer dans le Nord et L'Ouest de l'Europe jusqu'au XIIᵉ siècle," in *Ordinamenti militari in Occidente* (Spoleto, 1967), pp. 1009–63.

For the Hansa and the Baltic: P. Dollinger, *The German Hansa*, trans. D.S. Ault and S.H. Steinberg (Stanford, 1970), pp. 1–154; W. Urban, *The Baltic Crusade* (Dekalb, Illinois, 1975) and *The Prussian Crusade* (Lantham, Md., 1980) and *The Livonian Crusade* (Lantham, Md., 1981); H. Leach, *Angevin Britain and Scandinavia* (Cambridge, Mass., 1921); and A. Christensen, "La Foire de Scania" in *Recueils de la Société Jean Bodin* (Brussels, 1953). D. Bjork,

"Piracy in the Baltic, 1375–98," *Speculum* 18 (January 1943), pp. 39–68; M.M. Postan, "The Trade of Medieval Europe: The North," in *Cambridge Economic History*, II, eds. M.M. Postan and E.E. Rich (Cambridge, 1952), pp. 92–231.

For Atlantic Iberia: A. Lewis, "Northern European Sea-Power and the Strait of Gibraltar, 1031–1350" in *Order and Innovation in the Middle Ages*, W. Jordan, ed., Princeton, 1978); B. Diffie, *Prelude to Empire, Portugal Overseas before Henry the Navigator* (Lincoln, Neb., 1960); F. Perez-Embid, "Navigation et commerce dans le port de Séville au bas Moyen-Âge" in *Le Moyen Âge* 75, n. 2 (1969), pp. 263–89; n. 3, 479–502; P.E. Russell, *English Intervention in Spain and Portugal at the Time of Edward III and Richard II* (Oxford, 1955); C. Verlinden, *The Beginnings of Modern Colonization* (Ithaca, 1970); Robert S. Smith, *The Spanish Guild Merchant, A History of the Consulado, 1250–1700* (Durham, N.C., 1940).

For the North Atlantic, see V. Cassidy, *The Sea around Them* (Baton Rouge, 1965); and F. Gad, *The History of Greenland*, I (Montreal, 1971), pp. 1–152. For Norway see: Arnved Nedkvitne, "Handelssjøfarten Mellom Norge og England; høymiddelalderien," *Sjøfartshistorisk Arbok* (Norwegian Yearbook of Maritime History) (Bergen, 1976), pp. 1–254 dealing with ships and trade utilizing the English customs accounts and emphasizing Norwegian export of stockfish; K. Helle, "Trade and Shipping between Norway and England in the Reign of Hakon Hakonsson," *Sjøfartshistorisk Arbok* (Bergen, 1967) and his forthcoming *History of Bergen*. P. Heinsius, *Das Schiff der hansischen Frühzeit* (Weimar, 1956) is an important study.

On the law at sea: R.F. Wright, "The High Seas and the Church in the Middle Ages," *Mariner's Mirror* 53 (February, 1967), pp. 3–31; 53 (May, 1967), pp. 115–35; Timothy J. Runyan, "The Laws of Oléron and the Admiralty Court in Fourteenth Century England," *American Journal of Legal History*, xix (April, 1975) 95–111 and "Mariners and the Law of the Sea in Later Medieval England," *Gens de Mer en société*. Commission Internationale d'histoire maritime, ed. P. Adam (Paris, 1981), pp. 1–12; R.G. Marsden, *Documents Relating to the Law and Custom of the Sea, 1205–1648*, Vol. I, (London, 1915) and his *Select Pleas in the Court of Admiralty* (London, 1894); S.J. Jados, *Consulate of the Sea and Related Documents* (University, Alabama, 1975); T. Twiss, ed., *The Black Book of the Admiralty*, 4 vols. (London, 1871–76); W. McFee, *The Law of the Sea* (New York, 1950); H.S. Lucas, "John Crabbe: Flemish Pirate, Merchant and Adventurer," *Speculum* 20 (July 1945), pp. 334–50, provides one lawless example and see F.L. Cheyette, "The Sovereign and the Pirates, 1332," *Speculum* 45 (January 1970), pp. 40–68; C.L. Kingsford, "West Country Piracy: The School of English Seamen," in *Prejudice and Promise in Fifteenth Century England* (Oxford, 1925), pp. 78–106.

For Crusading and other voyages to and from the Mediterranean, see J. Shepard, "The English and Byzantium, a Study of Their Role in the Later Eleventh Century" in *Traditio* 29 (1975), pp. 53–92; T. Archer, *The Crusade of Richard I* (London, 1912); and E.B. Fryde, "Italian Maritime Trade with

England, c. 1270–1530" in *Recueils de la Société Jean Bodin* 36 (Brussels, 1974). Many pilgrimage accounts have been edited by the Palestine Pilgrim Texts Society. For a narrative account see H.F.M. Prescott, *Friar Felix at Large* (New Haven, 1950).

On ships in this era see J.W. Sherborne, "English Barges and Balingers of the Late Fourteenth Century," *Mariner's Mirror* 63 (May 1977), pp. 109–14; J.T. Tinniswood "English Galleys, 1272–1377," *Mariner's Mirror* 35 (October, 1949), pp. 276–315; R.J. Whitwell and C. Johnson, "The Newcastle Galley, A.D. 1294," *Archaeologia Aeliana*, 4th ser., 2 (1926), pp. 142–93; C. Johnson, "London Shipbuilding, A.D. 1295," *Antiquaries Journal* 7 (1927), pp. 424–37; R.C. Anderson, "English Galleys in 1295," *Mariner's Mirror* 35 (1949), pp. 220–41 For an English ship of note: S. Rose, "Henry V's *Grace Dieu* and Mutiny at Sea: Some New Evidence," *Mariner's Mirror* 63 (February 1977), pp. 3–6. On cogs see: O. Crumlin-Pedersen, "Cog-kogge-kaag. Trek af en frisisk skibstyper historie," *Handels-og Sjøfartsmuseet paa kronborg Arbog* (Copenhagen, 1965), pp. 82–144, which stresses the Frisian origin and hull shape of the cog. D. Ellmers, "The Cog of Bremen and Related Boats," in *Medieval Ships and Harbours in Northern Europe*, ed. S. McGrail (Oxford, 1979), pp. 1–16; S. Fliedner, "Die Bremer Kogge," Hefte des Focke–Museums Bremen II (1964) and *The Cog of Bremen* (Bremen, 1972). On nautical terminology and sources: B. Sandahl, *Middle English Sea Terms*, 3 vols. (Uppsala, 1954–82), an excellent study based on manuscript sources; I. Friel, "Documentary Sources and the Medieval Ship: Some Aspects of the Evidence," *International Journal of Nautical Archaeology* 12 (1983), pp. 41–62 and "England and the Advent of the Three-masted Ship," *Proceedings of the 4th International Congress of Maritime Museums* (Paris, 1981); S. Rose, *The Navy of the Lancastrian Kings: Accounts and Inventories of William Soper, Keeper of the King's Ships, 1422–27* (London, 1982); M. Oppenheim, *Naval Accounts and Inventories of the Reign of Henry VII: 1485–8 and 1495–7* (London, 1896). For the Dutch see: R.W. Unger, *Dutch Shipbuilding before 1800* (Amsterdam, 1978); R. Reinders, "Medieval Ships: Recent Finds in the Netherlands," in *Medieval Ships and Harbours in Northern Europe*, ed. S. McGrail (Oxford, 1979), pp. 35–44. For the French galleys see: A. Merlin-Chezelas, *Documents relatifs au clos des galées de Rouen*, 2 vols. (Paris, 1977–78).

CHAPTER VII.
THE RISE OF IBERIAN SEA POWER AND
A NEW ATLANTIC DESTINY, 1377–1498

The basic studies are: G.V. Scammel, *The World Encompassed: The First European Maritime Empires, c. 800–1650* (Berkeley, 1981); R.W. Unger, *The Ship in the Medieval Economy*, pp. 201–250; and J. Munro, *Wool, Cloth and Gold. The Struggle for Bullion in Anglo–Burgundian Trade, 1340–1478* (Toronto, 1972); J.H. Parry, *The Age of Reconnaissance* (New York, 1953); P. Chaunu, *European Expansion in the Later Middle Ages* (Amsterdam, 1978);

G.J. Marcus, *The Conquest of the North Atlantic* (Woodbridge, 1980); J.H. Parry, *The Discovery of the Sea* (London, 1974); and C. Cipolla, *Guns and Sails in the Early Phase of European Expansion, 1400–1700* (New York, 1965); F. Braudel, *The Mediterranean and the Mediterranean World in the Age of Philip II* 2 vols. (New York, 1973).

Other important works dealing with Iberia are: P. Russell, *Prince Henry the Navigator* (London, 1960); C. Verlinden, *La découverte des archipels de la Méditerranée Atlantique (Canaries, Madères, Açores) et la navigation astronomique primitive* (Coimbra, 1978); C.R. Boxer, *The Portuguese Seaborne Empire* (London, 1962), pp. 1–132; W.R. Childs, *Anglo-Castilian Trade in the Later Middle Ages* (Manchester, 1977); and M. Mallet, *Florentine Galleys in the Fifteenth Century* (Oxford, 1967); A.G. Sanz, ed. *Historia de la Marine Catalonia* (Barcelona, 1977); H. and P. Chaunu, *Séville et la Atlantique (1504–1650)*, 8 vols. (Paris, 1955–59); F.C. Lane, "Naval Actions and Fleet Organization, 1499–1502," in *Renaissance Venice*, ed. J.R. Hale (London, 1973), pp. 146–73.

For England, see D. Burwash, *English Merchant Shipping, 1460–1540* (Toronto, 1947); A.R. Bridbury, *England and the Salt Trade in the Later Middle Ages* (Oxford, 1955); E. Power and M. Postan, *Studies in English Trade in the Fifteenth Century* (London, 1933); P. Ramsay, "Overseas Trade in the Reign of Henry VII: The Evidence of Customs Accounts," in *Economic History Review*, 2nd ser., 6 (1953–4), pp. 173–82; and E.B. Fryde, "Anglo-Italian Commerce in the Fifteenth Century" in *Revue Belge* 50 (1972); A. Ruddock, *Italian Merchants and Shipping in Southampton 1270–1600* (Southampton, 1951); G.V. Scammel, "War at Sea Under the Early Tudors: Some Newcastle Upon Tyne Evidence," *Archaeologia Aeliana* 38 (1960), pp. 73–97; 39 (1961), pp. 179–205, and "English Merchant Shipping at the End of the Middle Ages: Some East Coast Evidence," *Economic History Review*, 2nd ser. 13 (April, 1961), pp. 327–41; G.J. Marcus, *A Naval History of England*, vol. 1 (London, 1961); the pamphlet by E.B. Fowler, *English Sea Power in the Early Tudor Period, 1485–1588* (Ithaca, 1965); M. Oppenheim wrote the maritime chapters in the *Victoria History of the Counties of England* (V.C.H.) and *A History of the Administration of the Royal Navy and of Merchant Shipping in Relation to the Navy from 1509 to 1660* (London, 1896) with an important first chapter; G.W. Warner, ed., *The Libelle of Englyshe Polyce. A Poem on the Use of Sea Power, 1439* (Oxford, 1926) and G.A. Holmes, "The Libel of English Policy," *English Historical Review* 76 (April 1961), pp. 193–216 who dates it c. 1436–38.

For the Netherlands: R. Vaughan, *Philip the Good. The Apogee of Burgundy* (London, 1970); R.W. Unger, "Dutch Ship Design in the Fifteenth and Sixteenth Centuries" in *Viator* IV (1973), pp. 387–412; and H. Van Der Wee, *The Growth of the Antwerp Market and the European Economy*, 3 vols. (The Hague, 1963).

For France: J. Bernard, *Navires et gens de mer à Bordeaux (vers 1400–vers 1550)*, 3 vols. (Paris, 1968); M. Mollat, *Le commerce maritime Normande à la fin du Moyen Âge* (Paris, 1952); and H. Touchard, *Le commerce maritime*

Breton à la fin du Moyen Âge (Paris, 1967); A. Hughet, *Aspects de la guerre de Cent Ans en Picardie Maritime*, 2 vols. (Amiens, 1941, 1944); and M. Mollat, *La Vie quotidienne des gens de mer en Atlantique, IXe–XVIe siècle* (Paris, 1983).

For the Baltic and Scandinavia: P. Dollinger, *The German Hansa*, ch. 10; and M. Malowist, "L'approvisionnement des ports de la Baltique en produits forestiers pour les constructions navales aux XVe et XVIe siècles" in *Travaux de Colloque International d'Histoire Maritime* III (Paris, 1960).

For Greenland and the Atlantic: F. Gad, *History of Greenland* I, pp. 153–195; and S.E. Morrison, *The European Discovery of America. The Northern Voyages, A.D. 500–1600* (New York, 1971) and *The European Discovery of America. The Southern Voyages, 1452–1616* (New York, 1971).

For navigation and maps: D.W. Waters, *Rutters of the Sea. The Sailing Directions of Pierre Garcie* (New Haven, 1967); E.G.R. Taylor, *The Haven-Finding Art. A History of Navigation* (New York, 1957); A.R. Lewis, "Maritime Skills in the Indian Ocean" in *The Sea and Medieval Civilizations* (London, 1980), pp. 251–53; and G.A. Crone, *Maps and Their Makers* (New York, 1962), pp. 25–78; A. Anthaume, *Cartes, Marines, Constructions navales et Voyages de découverte chez les normands*, 2 vols. (Paris, 1916); R. Mauny, *Les Navigations médiévales sur les côtes sahariennes antérieures à la découverte Portugaise* (Lisbon, 1960).

For the ship and technology see: R.M. Nance, "The Ship of the Renaissance," *Mariner's Mirror* 41 (August, 1955), pp. 180–92; J.F. Guilmartin, *Gunpowder and Galleys. Changing Technology and Mediterranean Warfare at Sea* (Cambridge, 1974); F.C. Lane, "The Crossbow in the Nautical Revolution of the Middle Ages," in D. Herlihy et al., eds., *Economy, Society and Government in Medieval Italy. Essays in Memory of Robert L. Reynolds* (Kent, Ohio, 1969), pp. 161–72; W.J. Carpenter Turner, "The Building of the *Gracedieu, Valentine* and *Falconer* at Southampton, 1416–1420," *Mariner's Mirror*, 40 (1954), 55–72 and "The Building of the *Holy Ghost of the Tower*, 1414–1416, and Her Subsequent History," ibid., 40 (1954), 270–81; R.W. Unger, "Warships and Cargo Ships," *Technology and Culture* 22 (April, 1981), pp. 233–52; José Martinez-Hidalgo, *Columbus' Ships* (Barre, Mass., 1977); Alexander McKee, "The Influence of British Naval Strategy on Ship Design: 1400–1850," *History of Seafaring Based on Underwater Archaeology*, ed. G. Bass (London, 1972), pp. 225–252; M.L. Peterson, "Traders and Privateers across the Atlantic," ibid., pp. 253–80; M. Rule, *The Mary Rose* (London, 1972).

Index